"Incisive, smart and incredibly fun . . . an ins~~~~~~~~~~~~~
aspiring screenwriters. This book is destined~~~~~~~~~~~~~~~~~~~~~~
and will sit next to *Adventures in the Screen* ~~~~~ and *Save the Cat* as the gold
standard on how to get your script written, sold, and most importantly: made."

—Richard Shepard, writer/director (*The Matador; Dom Hemingway; The Perfection*)

"Diamond and Weissman have written the ultimate how-to guide for writing
inside the studio system with lessons that can only be learned from years of
experience on the front lines and at the highest levels. This book contains all
the things an aspiring writer needs to know that they will not be taught in film
school."

—Sean Perrone manager, Kaplan/Perrone Entertainment

"A practical, funny, and down-to-Earth insider's guide that covers everything
from script development to what it's really like working in "the industry" —
from people who have actually done it."

—Etan Cohen, writer, (*Idiocracy; Tropic Thunder; Men in Black 3*)

"I love this book. Truly. It's like having lunch with David and David, albeit with
charts and one-pagers mixed in with the hummus and salad."

—Sascha Penn, writer (*Creed 2; Power*)

"Finally a screenwriting book by two incredibly talented, accomplished people
on the front lines who've actually written hit movies."

—Peter Steinfeld, writer (*21; Be Cool; Drowning Mona; Analyze That*)

"I reallllly wish I'd had this book when I started writing. It would have saved me
years of figuring it out."

—Will Akers, Chair and head of screenwriting, Curb College of Entertainment & Music
Business, Belmont University

"Diamond & Weissman are like talmudic brain surgeons when it comes to
screenwriting. Thankfully, they've put all their wisdom into this amazing book,
which is way better than any other screenwriting book."

—Roger Kumble writer, director (*Cruel Intentions; The Sweetest Thing*)

"Diamond and Weissman have a unique style that uses the head and the heart
to create stories that are universal and irresistible."

—Jon Shestack, producer (*Air Force One; Dan In Real Life*)

"The Davids have written an accessible, relatable and indispensable guide to
how to take a story from nascent idea to a great screenplay. No matter your
level of experience, it's a must read for anyone who cares about story."

—Jonathan Glickman, president, MGM Motion Picture Group

"As screenwriters, Diamond & Weissman possess the rare talent of being able to write from the heart — and in *Bulletproof* they reveal their process in a pragmatic way that any writer, novice or experienced, can benefit from."

—Jonathan Mostow, writer/director (*Breakdown; U-571; Terminator 3: Rise of the Machines*)

"(*Bulletproof*) changed the way I think about my screenwriting. A must read for every screenwriter, from the novice to the professional."

—Jonathan Fernandez, writer (*Rob the Mob),* Writers Guild of America Board of Directors

"The mix of practical but savvy, easy to understand advice and personal insights is both extraordinarily educational but surprisingly encouraging. I recommend this book for screenwriters at any level."

—David J. Greenberg, University of the Arts/Drexel University

"I loved it! I read it in one sitting. It's so honest. I think it would be really helpful for anyone daring to enter. . . . it made me want to write a script."

—Holly Bario, president of production, DreamWorks Studios

"The book is filled with nuggets to hone your skills and make your script bulletproof, so that you can thrive and succeed in the network, studio, and streaming universes."

—Dr. Selise E. Eiseman, screenwriter and film and education professor

"What's so incredible about *Bulletproof* is that it's as 'inside' a book about writing Hollywood scripts as has been written. I love the Davids, and I love their book."

—Bert Salke, president Fox 21 Television Studios

"The closest I've found to the 'secret sauce' that can help get scripts sold and produced."

—Elliot Grove, founder, Raindance Film Festival & British Independent Film Awards

They say write what you know. But as I know incredibly little, thank the lord Diamond & Weissman have written this book. I truly wish I had it when I was starting out."

—David Berenbaum, writer (*Elf; The Haunted Mansion; The Spiderwick Chronicles*)

"Where was *Bulletproof* when I needed it? Oh, wait I still need it! A great how-to for the first-time writer; an equally essential refresher for the veteran."

—John Eisendrath, co-creator (*The Blacklist*), writer-producer (*Alias*)

"Before I was even halfway through, I began applying their techniques to make my next script bulletproof. Their advice is so good, they may try to commission me ten percent!"

—Chris Brancato, co-creator and showrunner (*Narcos; Godfather of Harlem*)

DAVID DIAMOND | DAVID WEISSMAN

bullet proof

Writing Scripts That Don't Get Shot Down

MICHAEL WIESE PRODUCTIONS

Published by Michael Wiese Productions
12400 Ventura Blvd. #1111
Studio City, CA 91604
(818) 379-8799, (818) 986-3408 (Fax)
mw@mwp.com
www.mwp.com
Manufactured in the
United States of America

This book was set in Garamond Premier Pro and Gotham

Cover design by Johnny Ink. johnnyink.com
Interior design by Debbie Berne
Copyediting by Sherry Parnes

Library of Congress Cataloging-in-Publication Data

Names: Diamond, David, 1965- author. | Weissman, David, author.
Title: Bulletproof: writing scripts that don't get shot down /
    by David Diamond & David Weissman.
Description: Studio City, CA: Michael Wiese Productions, [2019] |
    Includes bibliographical references.
Identifiers: LCCN 2018043047 | ISBN 9781615932993
Subjects: LCSH: Motion picture authorship—Vocational guidance.
Classification: LCC PN1996 .D485 2019 | DDC 808.2/3—dc23
LC record available at https://lccn.loc.gov/2018043047

To our wives, Audrey and Diane,
and the kids,
Hannah, Harry, and Benjamin, Ike and Oren.

If not for you
Winter would have no spring
Couldn't hear the robin sing
I just wouldn't have a clue
Anyway it wouldn't ring true
If not for you
—Bob Dylan

contents

preface

This book is the product of about five hundred cups of coffee. That is, give or take a few dozen cups, the amount of caffeine the two of us have ingested over the past twenty-five years, meeting with aspiring screenwriters to share our experience and provide guidance, support, or advice. At a certain point, about a year ago, it occurred to us to put as much as we could of what we tended to share with others in one place, where it could be accessible to anyone who may be interested; all for the relatively low cost of a few Grande Frappuccinos.

We are not screenwriting teachers or story gurus. We're not academics or experts on dramaturgy, mythology and archetypes, film theory or analysis. We're screenwriters. We write movies. Some get made, some don't. We write original scripts, we adapt books. We work on assignment and we sell pitches. We start at the very beginning, from the very first spark of an idea, and we come in at the end, providing a week or more of production polish to scripts that are getting made as a result of years of work by other writers, sometimes numerous other writers. The movies we've worked on, credited and uncredited, over the course of our career have earned over a billion dollars worldwide. We're part of a small cadre of proud, if not particularly influential, screenwriters whose careers have endured and thrived well into a third decade. In that time, we've accumulated a considerable amount of practical experience and we've developed a writing process that's been helpful to us and effective at getting us, in the best cases, from that first spark of creative inspiration through production. It's that process, and the bulletproof approach that's evolved along with it, that we're sharing now in the form of this practical guide.

What do we mean by "bulletproof?"

Put simply, the bulletproof approach is about getting to "yes" in a town where everyone — agents, producers, executives, even script readers — is predisposed to saying no. It's a way to view every stage of the writing process, from concept to final polish, from the perspective of the folks you're trying to sell to, thus avoiding some of the most common pitfalls and barriers to entry. It's a way of approaching screenwriting that recognizes upfront how collaborative a process moviemaking is, and views the discerning eyes of future partners as necessary and helpful pieces in a common creative pursuit. And it's never been more essential than it is today.

The market for spec scripts and original movies is more challenging now than it has been in all the years we've been in the business. Back in the 1990's, when we were starting out, scripts were selling for multiple millions of dollars, oftentimes more than one in a given week. The trades, *Daily Variety* and *The Hollywood Reporter* (this was pre-*Deadline*; pre-internet in fact), were filled with announcements of spec sales from new and established writers — Shane Black, Joe Eszterhas, Ron Bass. Our first spec sale was one of them.* If you follow *Deadline* now, or any of the other industry sites, you'll notice that it's become relatively rare to see news of a spec or pitch sale. More common is the announcement of which established writer has been assigned the latest installment of this or that effects-driven franchise. Anything less than a bulletproof spec is immediately shot down.

A 2013 article in *Vanity Fair* summed up the downward trend in spec sales with this startling statistic, "In 1995, 173 specs were sold. In 2010 the number was 55, roughly where it had stood for at least half a decade."** And that was 2013. The trend toward movies based on previously existing material, intellectual property — comic books, television series, video games, old movies that can be remade, and barely cold franchises rebooted — and away from original material has only continued and grown in the years since. Even streaming services, which offer promising new opportunities, seek content adapted from familiar

---

* "Wood in as Fox's 'Whiz Kid'" by Michael Fleming, *Daily Variety* March 28, 1994.
** "When the Spec Script was King" by Margaret Heidenry, *Vanity Fair*, February 8, 2013.

sources and big packages — filmmakers and stars — to drive interest in their product and attract viewers. Still, the truth is that the spec screenplay remains the best way for an aspiring screenwriter to gain entry into the movie business. Even successful, seasoned writers are turning to packaging spec scripts to get original movies made. And yet, it's harder than ever to get the attention of agents, producers, studio executives, and other buyers. What do you do? How do you understand the critical difference between a screenplay that can advance your career and one that gathers dust on a shelf? What does it take to bridge that gap? These are the questions this book will help you answer.

A general note on screenwriting books. With the exception of William Goldman's classic *Adventures in the Screen Trade*, we didn't read them until we started to write one of our own. Most of them seem to have something to offer — insightful analyses of movies that have gotten it right and wrong, practical suggestions, strategies for getting from start to finish and confronting the rough patches that inevitably occur in between, elaborate theories of storytelling and structure that may have merit and prove helpful. The guides written by working screenwriters with produced studio credits are fewer and farther between, and they are qualitatively different. Read *Save the Cat* by Blake Snyder and *Writing Movies for Fun and Profit* by Lennon and Garant. And, of course, Goldman's gold standard, which still holds up almost thirty years later. These books are generally more practical than the "systems" and theories of narrative construction developed by structure gurus and academics. Their approach tends to reflect the way scripts actually attract the attention of buyers and progress toward production. This book is intended to add to that conversation.

That said, use whatever helps. There's no magic formula, and no one expert — including us — has all the answers. Be very skeptical of anyone who tells you otherwise, who guarantees success if you just follow their "simple steps." The only one who can get you where you want to go in your writing is you. We're just trying to help.

Is this book for everybody? Probably not. Legend has it The Rolling

Stones' "(I Can't Get No) Satisfaction" came to Keith Richards in a dream. He woke up, put the guitar riff down on a cassette player, and went back to sleep. Mick Jagger wrote the lyrics in ten minutes the next day, sitting by a motel pool. That's the second-best rock and roll song of all time, after Dylan's "Like a Rolling Stone," according to *Rolling Stone* magazine. We can quibble about the rankings, but that's not the point. The point is, we're not all Keith Richards and Mick Jagger. We don't all wake up in the middle of the night with the hook for one of the greatest songs ever written in our head and have the benefit of a writing partner who can put just the right lyrics to it in ten minutes sitting poolside at a Florida motel. Some people just seem to have a gift for conceiving fresh ideas and knowing exactly how to render them most effectively. But most of us mortals need a process we can rely on over time to coax our most creative impulses out of us, provide the discipline to execute them in the best possible way, and avoid the pitfalls that can doom our work in the eyes of Hollywood.

Having a specific method you can count on — that you can use over and over — might sound constraining, even antithetical to the creative process. Or maybe you imagine it's something that you use only in the very beginning, when you're first learning the craft, that becomes obsolete after you've made that first big spec sale and demonstrated that you know what you're doing. We tend to think of it more like batting practice in the major leagues. Integrating a specific, consistent process into your writing routine doesn't guarantee you'll knock it out of the park every time you step up to the plate, but you stand a helluva better chance than the batter who sits it out, choosing instead to rely solely on raw talent. As Malcolm Gladwell argues in his book *Outliers*, none of us, not even the geniuses among us, gets there on talent alone.* Success requires both talent and a process, a regimen of regular and deliberate practice, at least 10,000 hours in Gladwell's estimation. That 10,000 hours of practice and process is your apprenticeship. It's a time for

---

* *Outliers* by Malcolm Gladwell, Chapter Two "The 10,000-Hour Rule"

taking risks, making mistakes, honing your craft, and learning where and how you fit into the special world you aspire to enter. There are no shortcuts, but you can learn from other people's experience and from their mistakes, and we have plenty of both to share.

Kurt Vonnegut Jr. once wrote, "If a person with a demonstrably ordinary mind, like mine, will devote himself to giving birth to a work of the imagination, that work will in turn tempt and tease that ordinary mind into cleverness."* Devoting yourself, that's the key. After all, even Keith Richards took guitar lessons.

* Kurt Vonnegut Jr. *Wampeters, Foma & Granfalloons (Opinions)* Preface, 1974

introduction

Think about yourself and the other aspiring writers you know. Most go from concept to completed screenplay without ever stopping to consider the reality of all that has to happen for that script to actually sell. What exactly has to happen?

First, you need to get your script into the hands of someone who can actually do something for you, even if "doing something for you" merely means passing your script along to someone else who can do something for you. Let's just pause a moment to consider that. Think of someone you know, or know of, who might be in a position to help advance your script. It could be a friend or relative, could be someone you've worked for at an agency or production company, someone you've met socially, or an industry professional you've been put in touch with through a mutual friend or acquaintance. What motivates them to hand your script to an agent, producer, or executive and say, "You have to read this!"? It's a rhetorical question. We're actually going to tell you the answer. The answer is that passing along your script has to reflect well on them. It has to benefit them.

This is a business, not a fairy tale or a family reunion. Nobody in the movie business recommends a screenplay with the sole intention of helping a writer realize their dreams. They pass along a screenplay because doing so will reflect well on them and possibly benefit them in some way — either because the script is great or because it's enormously commercial, ideally both. In a business built on relationships and reputations, where there's too much material and not enough time to process and evaluate it all, it is absolutely essential to be discriminating. You may be wrong. The number of people who rejected the script for *Star Wars* has become the stuff of legend. But you still have to be discriminating. You can only recommend the material you genuinely believe in, the writers you can truly get behind. If people disagree, they disagree. But if they think you're just submitting a script for the hell of it, because your nephew wrote it, then you've taken them and their time for granted, you lose your credibility, and that avenue will no longer be open to you, or to any writer who hopes to gain access through you.

This is the case with the first person you hand your script to, and with every person who follows them in the Hollywood chain. Now consider the chain. An agent or manager has to read your script and say, "It will benefit me to give this to a producer." The producer then has to read it and say, "It will benefit me to give this to X or Y director." The director has to read it and say "It will benefit me to spend a year or two of my life making this movie, or at the very least to expend some capital at the studio to attach myself and develop it." Then the studio executive has to read it and say, "It will benefit me to invest our limited time and development dollars in this script with this director and this producer," . . . and on and on and on. You get the idea.

We can mix up the elements in a hundred different ways but, at the end of the day, selling screenplays is essentially an extended game of *It will benefit me.* If you've ever believed Hollywood exists to make your dreams come true you should dispense with that notion right now. The first step in writing the bulletproof screenplay is recognizing that just the opposite is true. It's the writer who takes it upon him or herself to make everyone else's dreams come true. That is, more often than not, the way scripts get sold and produced.

So it's on you to deliver a piece of material that will move and benefit everyone else in the Hollywood chain — an agent or manager, a producer, a director, an actor, and a studio or financier — when every link in that chain represents another possibility and threat of a "PASS." That's what this book, and the bulletproof approach, is about — scrutinizing every choice from the perspective of story and character *and through the lens of the folks who will need to say "YES" and come aboard to turn your vision into a reality.*

In the following chapters, we'll call on our experience with our own projects, as well as other familiar movies, to guide you through the process of fashioning a screenplay that concerns itself with good ideas and storytelling, adhering to the conventions of Hollywood story structure, and also takes into account the extent to which that screenplay must serve the needs and interests of all the various creative and financial stakeholders in the movie.

The time we've spent, and the hundreds of cups of coffee we've consumed in conversation with aspiring writers over the years, is a perk of the job. Sometimes there's a follow-up coffee, a continuing conversation. Most often, though, it's an hour or two of sharing our experience and perspective, and then we part ways. With this book, we're sticking with you, the writer, the whole way; from the germ of your idea, through your outline or treatment, to your finished screenplay and beyond. This book is the bottomless cup of coffee that hopes to meet you as a writer with a dream, and not leave you until you're a member of the community of working screenwriters. To do that, we're going to have to go well beyond simply completing your script. We're going to have to examine every aspect of your idea, your process, and your screenplay, and make sure they're Bulletproof (trademark, patent pending). Together, we're going to disarm the naysayers by building your story and fashioning your screenplay in a way that anticipates their needs and concerns, captures their imaginations, and inspires their enthusiasm. This is what the business requires of us all, especially today. It is, we believe, an investment well worth making. After all, what good is writing a movie in 90, 30, or even 21 days if no one buys it?

the bulletproof movie idea

Writing a movie you hope to sell and proceed to production is like running a gauntlet, like Luke Skywalker and the Rebel Alliance trying to destroy the Death Star at the end of *Star Wars*. At any given moment, a new obstacle can emerge, stopping you in your tracks, or sending you right back to square one. Luke's best and only hope in *Star Wars* was The Force. Yours is a great movie idea. It's been said that you can make a bad movie from a good script but you cannot make a good movie from a bad script. And you certainly can't write a good script from a bad idea, or from no idea at all. So it's important to understand, before you proceed any further in the process, what a viable movie idea is, and how to formulate an idea that is not just serviceable, but really good, or great . . . or bulletproof.

Who's to say whether your idea is the greatest to come along since *Citizen Kane* or the worst since 2004's *Sex Lives of the Potato Men*? Isn't that an entirely subjective distinction? The answer is yes and no. Of course it's subjective, and there will always be people who respond to your ideas with greater and lesser degrees of enthusiasm. But the market has a voice and a vote, too. And it's an important one. After all, you want to sell your script, right? And selling your script requires a buyer. Does every movie that sells and gets made have a great idea behind it? No. If you don't sell your script, does that necessarily mean your idea sucks? Of course not. Screenwriting and script sales are not a science and there are no absolutes. That said, in our experience and for our practical purposes, a good idea is one that will turn the heads of agents and producers and directors and actors and financiers. It's an idea that will advance your script and your career. The bulletproof screenplay is one that presents its reader with a clear path to production. That path will inevitably be riddled with obstacles, setbacks, and detours, some of them potentially insurmountable. That is precisely why your experienced reader is looking for the best odds going in.

As we're reminded all the time when vetting our own ideas, there's a big difference between, *Yeah, I get it,* and *I've gotta have it. Yeah, I get it* is the response to a potentially viable, but familiar idea. *Yeah, I get it* doesn't pay the bills. In fact, it really doesn't get you anywhere, except perhaps another bite at the apple somewhere down the line, if you're lucky. *I've gotta have it!* can start your career, and if you deliver on the screenplay, it will likely start it in fifth gear. A bulletproof movie idea — one that cannot be shot down — is harder to find than one might imagine. Let's explore the difference in these various gradations of movie ideas, what goes into them, and how to make the one you choose to invest your time and energy into bulletproof.

The Difference Between an Idea for a Movie and an Idea for a Screenplay

One thing many less experienced, and even some more experienced screenwriters sometimes fail to appreciate is that there's a difference between an idea for a screenplay and an idea for a movie. A typical screenplay runs between 90 and 120 pages that are formatted in a particular way. In theory, if you downloaded Final Draft, the industry standard screenwriting app (which you should), and simply wrote a few scenes every day involving the same cast of characters, writing whatever happened to inspire you until you hit page 100, you could reasonably say you'd completed your first screenplay. But have you written a movie? Not likely.

Writing a screenplay from a great idea may sound simple — so simple, in fact, that many who have never, and will never actually sit down to write a screenplay happen to think they have a *terrific* idea for a movie! But do they? If you listen to the stories of non-writers who tell you they have a great idea you'll often find that your friend, or relative, or the stranger you've just met in line at Trader Joe's who you were foolish enough to tell you were a writer, has mistaken something that happened to them or someone they know for a movie idea. An incident, no matter how significant it may be to you, is not a movie idea simply because it really happened. Might it be built into a movie idea? Possibly. That's where character and context, and a deeper understanding of the craft and the process, come in. It's where a writer comes in. But an episode from your life, in and of itself, is not a movie. The same can be said of the people you or your friends or relatives know. Your mother's Pilates instructor, your auto mechanic, the eccentric uncle who exudes personality . . . these folks may all be very entertaining and interesting people. They are not necessarily worthy and compelling subjects for your next movie.

So how much is enough? And how much is too much? Before you can make the idea for your movie bulletproof, you need to know how much information, and specifically *what* information you need. What actually constitutes a movie idea?

Think of your movie idea like an atom, the building block of all matter. Just as you have no solid, liquid, or gas without atoms, you have no movie without an idea at its center. But atoms themselves consist of smaller components — protons, neutrons and electrons.* Similarly, your movie idea, the foundation of all the work you will do and the pages you will produce, has three essential components — a character, a concept, and a context. A complete movie idea is: this person, in that situation, under these circumstances. Character. Concept. Context.

Anatomy of a Movie Idea: The Three C's

Like protons, neutrons and electrons in the atom, these three component parts — concept, character, and context — are each so integral to your movie idea that it's nearly impossible to evaluate the merits of any one without considering the others. Let's take the seminal 1993 comedy *Groundhog Day* as an example. *Groundhog Day* is about a guy who lives the same day over and over again. That's the idea, right? Well, no. That's only part of the idea. That's the concept. And it's a good one — at least it was in 1993. A movie concept is a *situation* that poses a significant, high-stakes challenge or opportunity to your lead character or ensemble. A character who's forced to live the same day over and over is a promising concept, it's a good jumping off point for a movie idea. But does the concept alone, the situation, tell you what kind of movie it is? Not really. It could be the basis of a sci-fi film, a horror film, a thriller, a comedy. Who's the star in this situation, a comedian, a dramatic actor, or an action star? If you were trying to cast the movie today based on concept alone, without any other information to go on,

---

* With apologies to Ira Stern, our 10th grade chemistry teacher, this is the extent of our knowledge of basic chemistry.

your lead could be Kevin Hart or it could be Liam Neeson. Those are two very different movies. If you were making it with a woman in the lead it could be Melissa McCarthy or Charlize Theron, depending on the character and context.

Now let's add the character from the actual movie, a perpetually dissatisfied Pittsburgh weatherman. A perpetually dissatisfied weatherman who lives the same day over and over suggests a comic character in what I now glean to be a comic situation. Pittsburgh tells me he's local. Perpetually dissatisfied suggests he'd rather be working in, and believes himself worthy of, a larger market, like L.A. or New York, and probably in a more prestigious position, a news anchor perhaps. Groundhog Day provides not just the title, but the context. It's February 2nd, the day on the annual calendar when throngs of people gather in Punxsutawney, Pennsylvania to see the groundhog and learn if winter is going to extend or spring will come early. So if you're Danny Rubin, the original writer of *Groundhog Day*, and Aunt Irma asks at Thanksgiving dinner what the project you're working on is about, you might say, "It's about a perpetually dissatisfied local weatherman who's sent to cover the annual Groundhog Day celebration in Punxsutawney, Pennsylvania and ends up stuck in town, living the same day over and over again until he gets it right."

That gives me pretty much all the information I need to tell if this is a script I'd be interested in reading. I know, first of all, that it's a comedy. I can tell this from the character, the location, and the choice of Groundhog Day as the story trigger. If it was Friday the 13th, for example, that would leave a very different impression. If it was the day the protagonist's wife died, I'd assume something else entirely. I know that being stuck in a small town in Western Pennsylvania is pretty much the last thing a perpetually dissatisfied local weatherman would want to have happen to him, which tells me this is a good situation to challenge the lead character in the movie. We'll talk more about character later, in Chapter Four, but for the purpose of framing your idea, the lead character or ensemble you want is one who will be most challenged or rewarded by the situation you've conceived, and one we want to follow from the beginning of your story through to the end. This dissatisfied weatherman sounds like the right character, or at the very least a very good choice for a character stuck in Punxsutawney, living the same day over and over again. Finally, I know from the last phrase, "until he gets it right" that this character is going to change in some way as a result of being stuck here. I might not know precisely what that change is or how it's going to happen. That's good. For now, when I consider the idea for *Groundhog Day*, I just want to know that there's movement in the story, growth in the character, and I want to have a sense of the tone. *Groundhog Day* places a good, fun character in a challenging situation, in a context that suggests just the right kind of opportunity for change and resolution. I'd like to read that. More important, I'd like to see that. *Groundhog Day* was a bulletproof idea.

Here's one of our favorite movie ideas from early in our own career. *Guam Goes to the Moon* is about a maverick astronaut, expelled by NASA, who's recruited by a billionaire from the U.S. territory of Guam to put the tiny island on the map by leading a moonshot in an old Russian N-1 rocket.

What do we know from this idea? We know our lead character has something to prove, to himself and maybe to the world. He didn't live up to his potential at NASA. We know he's being offered a second chance in the form of this moonshot, which represents a bigger dream and accomplishment than even NASA could have offered him. But we also know that it's Guam, not exactly a world superpower, and that the Russians and their N-1 rocket lost the space race to the Americans and the Saturn 5. The old Russian rocket and the setting in the unincorporated U.S. island territory of Guam suggest an underdog comedy. And that's precisely what *Guam Goes to the Moon* was when we sold it on a pitch to 20th Century Fox in 1995 — an underdog comedy in the vein of *Cool Runnings*, *Bad News Bears*, or more recently, *Dodgeball* or Disney's *Million Dollar Arm*.

Guam Goes to the Moon currently sits on a shelf at Paramount

Pictures with hundreds of other unproduced screenplays. Does that mean it wasn't a bulletproof idea? You decide. We sold *Guam* as a pitch to one studio in 1995. It then moved with its producer to another studio, where we worked on it, on and off, for the next ten years. Over those years we worked on the script with five different producers and three different directors. Falling just short of a green light, time after time, is enormously frustrating and disappointing. But working on that project has also given us the opportunity to work with a number of really accomplished, talented people — directors, producers, executives — we'd otherwise never have met, and establish professional relationships we might otherwise never have formed. And we were paid. *Guam Goes to the Moon* helped pay our mortgages and put food on our tables. Every professional writer has screenplays on the shelf. In the end, some ideas and scripts prove to be more bulletproof than others. Timing and luck — serendipity — often plays as important a roll in the process, and the results, as merit. No writer makes everything — not unless they're financing all their own films. For now, let's just try to start with a good idea. No, not a good idea . . . a bulletproof idea.

Vetting Your Idea

So you have your concept, you know who your character is, and you know the larger circumstances that elevate your character and concept. You have your movie idea. How do you know if it's any good? How do you know if it's an idea people will be excited enough about to get off the couch, sign out of Netflix, close their Snapchat or Instagram . . . or Tinder, and actually head to a movie theater where they'll have to plop down their hard-earned cash to see your movie? You ask them. Seriously, if you want to know if there's an audience for your movie, you have to tell people what you're working on. At this point, some writers rush to craft the perfect "logline" for their idea. We would strongly urge you not to do that.

The Logline

A logline is a succinct, one or two sentence description of your screenplay or movie. The classic example, perhaps the origin, is *TV Guide*. Back when people actually subscribed to a printed magazine that told them what was on television, *TV Guide* provided a single line that teased just enough information about a movie or television show for the viewer to know if he or she was interested. Today, streaming services and the Guide feature on your cable or satellite TV menu also use loglines. Loglines are a useful and important tool, but they're for completed screenplays and movies, not for vetting ideas. And there are good reasons for that. First, we don't speak in loglines. If you were raving about the movie *Baby Driver* and your friend asked you what it was about, would you say, "After being coerced into working for a crime boss, a young getaway driver finds himself taking part in a heist doomed to fail?"* Probably not. It's not wrong, it's just not how human beings speak to each other in conversation. Loglines sound canned, and the last thing you want to do when you're vetting your idea, trying to get an enthusiastic reaction from friends or industry contacts, is talk about what you're working on in a way that sounds canned.

Second, writers who begin with the logline often invest way too much time and energy, subjecting themselves to all sorts of mental and written gymnastics, just to come up with that one perfect sentence. Trust us, what can take hours when you're at the beginning stages will take about thirty seconds after your idea is fully realized and your screenplay is written. In fact, the wrong or deficient logline can throw you off course. The process of figuring out your characters, and your story, going through an outline, and writing a screenplay, will reveal all sorts of things you cannot know yet about the relative weight of your characters and the prominence of different aspects of your story. It's possible that this will impact how you'd describe your finished

---

* Logline courtesy of IMDb: www.imdb.com/title/tt3890160/reference

screenplay or movie. Trying to encapsulate your movie idea in a logline at this stage in the process is a mistake, possibly even a trap you'll spend hours, days, or weeks trying to climb your way out of. Screenwriting is not a science, it's an art, a creative process. There's no need to turn this process into something contrived before you've even put pen to paper, making yourself feel like a failure just because you can't figure out yet how to sum up your idea in ten words or less. Don't waste your time with a logline now; save it for later.

Having said all that, you *do* need to be able to talk about what you're working on with people you know and trust and believe can be helpful. Not in loglines, but in a few simple, clear, conversational sentences that convey who your movie is about, and what happens to them under what circumstances. Just as we described earlier. If you're comfortable with your concept and your character, you should be able to communicate that succinctly and enthusiastically in conversation. Tell anyone who asks what you do, or what you're working on. Gauge their reaction. Do their eyes widen with enthusiasm and anticipation? Do they ask questions? Do they ask to hear more? Or do they say, *Oh, I get it,* and then quickly change the subject? Even a look that says, *Oh, I get it* can suggest that your idea might not spark the same interest in others that it does in you. Or maybe it's just a smaller, more life-size idea. If that's the case, you should be able to speak about your idea with a greater level of specificity that brings your more intimate idea to life. If that happens, you may still be in good shape. If it's not happening, you may not be sufficiently clear yet about the different aspects of your idea, or the idea itself may be lacking.

In either case: Do not pass go, do not collect $200. You probably have to dig deeper, or elsewhere. Our hope is that the following pages and chapters will help guide you.

Of course, telling people your idea means . . . telling people your idea. And some writers are understandably skittish about revealing their ideas for fear of having them stolen. First, don't flatter yourself. We hope your idea is great and wholly unique, the holy grail of movie ideas. More likely, there's one similar to it in development somewhere (maybe even one at every studio). That can be a problem if the idea and the rendering are too close to what's been done. But it doesn't necessarily have to be a problem. As Ecclesiastes wrote over two thousand years ago, "There's nothing new under the sun." Your finished screenplay should incorporate elements we've not seen before in the movies — visuals or language, characters or plot devices, a fresh perspective, ideas for comic set pieces or action sequences. It should be the kind of script financiers and marketing people will be interested in because they see a way to sell it to audiences. The idea you're looking for is one that provides an opportunity for unique execution, and the potential for an eager audience. But unique in some way does not mean unique in every way. In fact, unique in every way can also mean unrelatable, inaccessible, untethered . . . . Let's say, though, just for the sake of argument, that you have come up with something truly original. Let's say you're Lilly & Lana Wachowski and you've just birthed the idea for *The Matrix* (which is really a repackaged version of the classic hero's journey story). *The Matrix* is a prime example of *I've gotta have it.* Do you really think that anyone but the Wachowskis could have executed the idea for *The Matrix* in the way that they did? Don't worry so much about people stealing your ideas. It's your idea, you came up with it. If you're half the writer you think you are, no one else out there will be able to render it as you would, in that *I've gotta have it* way.*

What if you don't get an enthusiastic response to your idea? What if you don't even get a lukewarm response? Should you assume that people "just don't get it," that they don't appreciate your unique talents and ability to execute, and persist? Mmm . . . probably not. Not with this idea. Even worse than *Yeah, I get it* is *Sorry, I don't get it.* Trust us, we know this from personal experience. If you're Spike Jonze or Charlie

---

* That said, once you've got a good synopsis of your screenplay on paper, let's be safe and register that idea with the Writers Guild of America at www.wgawregistry.org, shall we?

Kaufman, *I don't get it* might not scare you. Ever seen *Synecdoche, New York*? But if you're like us, and you aspire to write accessible movies aimed to appeal to larger audiences, *I don't get it* is not a great sign. It means that either you haven't figured out how to communicate your idea effectively or there's something about the idea itself that doesn't quite add up. In either case, you have to go back to the drawing board and figure that out. Presumably, if you've made a decision to make a go of screenwriting, you have some kind of creative community of support around you — a writing group, people who work in the industry, friends from work you talk about movies with, family members. If you don't, you should. You want these people to be excited about what you're working on, just as you are. You may even want them to read pages as you write. J.K. Rowling said, "No story lives unless someone wants to listen." If the idea you're pursuing appeals only to you and no one else, it's hard to see how that can be a worthwhile investment of your time. If you don't have any kind of creative community around you and you're serious about trying to become a screenwriter, you should find one. Or move. Seriously. It's too hard to do this work, let alone succeed in it, in a vacuum. You need to be exposed to, and in conversation with, other creative people whose opinions and points of view you respect, whose companionship you value and enjoy. You need the help and support of people who really understand what it is you've undertaken.

If you've vetted your idea with the right people, and the right number of people, you'll notice that the bulletproof movie idea is not one that simply rehashes old concepts ("It's *The Hangover* for women . . . " "It's *Fast and the Furious* in space . . . !"). The best and most impactful ideas contribute something new to their genre, to the ongoing creative conversation that takes place in the movies. Think about Jordan Peele's *Get Out*, Diablo Cody's *Juno*, Judd Apatow's *40 Year-Old Virgin*. All originals. These are "water cooler movies," in addition to being significant hits. They created buzz. Does *Thor: Ragnarock* contribute to the creative conversation of the movies? Maybe not as much. But you're not going to get the job writing that movie, certainly not before you've turned some heads with a bulletproof original screenplay. Why did Rian Johnson get the job writing and directing *Star Wars: The Last Jedi*, Episode VIII in the franchise, which grossed over a billion dollars in less than two weeks? Because he wrote and directed a really cool, attention grabbing *original* movie called *Looper* five years earlier. This is the value and the importance of your bulletproof original, and it begins with your idea.

So there's a bit of a double standard. Hollywood is desperate for proven concepts and properties, things we've seen before, that are familiar and therefore easier and less expensive to market. But Hollywood is not looking for that from *you*, the aspiring writer. From you, Hollywood is looking for a fresh new voice . . . that they can then hire to write installments of familiar franchises. Michael Arndt wrote *Little Miss Sunshine*, one of the freshest and most satisfying independent films of the last twenty years. That was his first produced screenplay, an original. He also wrote *Toy Story 3*, which was inspired, inspiring and fabulous, and *Star Wars: The Force Awakens*. So, yeah . . . there's something a little hypocritical about Hollywood. Studios are looking for the fresh and the familiar at the very same time. If this bothers or confounds you, get over it. Being bitter and resentful and contrary only creates one more barrier to entry — your own attitude. And there are enough barriers to entry as it is, you do not need one more. Prove yourself by being fresh and original so that the powers-that-be might one day come to you asking for the safer and more familiar. We were asked to write a film adaptation of the television series *My Three Sons* because of the original script we wrote for *The Family Man*. It may be true that there's nothing new under the sun. That doesn't mean that a screenwriter working on assignment has to surrender creativity and originality. There's always a fresh, new and attention-grabbing way to approach something we've all seen before.

Finally, a word of encouragement. It took us five years before we had an idea that became a script that we could sell to a studio.

Those five years were our journey from *I don't get it,* past *Yeah, I get it,* until we finally reached *I've gotta have it.* We're trying to save you a little time by sharing our own experience and some insights we've gleaned along the way. The journey for you might take much less time, or it might take more. Pursue it as long as you love it, as long as you're drawn to it, and as long as you can do it responsibly without causing harm to yourself or others. The rewards when things finally click can be tremendously satisfying.

Finding Your Idea's Place in the Landscape: Studio vs. Indie Ideas

Does your movie idea have to be a giant, expensive, tent pole idea? No. It doesn't hurt, but no. A bold independent film script can do as much for your writing career as a spec for a big, expensive studio movie. See the above-mentioned examples, *Juno* and *Little Miss Sunshine* and *Looper.* Look at the writing careers of Kenneth Lonergan, Lena Dunham, and Tom McCarthy. So how do you know if the idea you've come up with, and the movie you want to write, is a studio movie or an independent film? Generally speaking, studio movies feature larger-than-life characters in larger-than-life situations. Think about *The Martian.* Matt Damon, a movie star, plays Mark Watney, an astronaut-scientist who is accidentally abandoned and left for dead by his crewmates on Mars as they're fleeing a deadly storm. He then engages in a race against the clock to communicate with NASA and devise a way to get off the Red Planet before he runs out of the resources he needs to survive. Now consider, by contrast, Ellen Page's character in *Juno,* written by Diablo Cody. Page, a relative newcomer and an unknown at the time of the film's release, plays offbeat 16 year-old high school student Juno MacGuff, who becomes pregnant as the result of a one-time sexual encounter with her friend Paulie Bleeker, played by Michael Cera. Juno decides to defy expectations and eschew aborting the pregnancy in favor of carrying the baby to term and turning it over to more suitable parents, played by Jason Bateman and Jennifer Garner. Complications ensue, but the situation and characters in *Juno* really are not at all larger than life. The story is witty and clever and emotionally rich, but it's quite life size. Juno's journey over the course of the movie wouldn't even merit a headline in the local newspaper, but the movie was a critical darling and an audience favorite. And Diablo Cody has gone on to a successful and enduring career writing for movies and television.

Lady Bird is another example. Saoirse Ronan plays the title character in the coming of age drama about an eccentric high school student in Sacramento who dreams of getting out, beginning with college. She has a deep and complicated relationship with her mother, played by Laurie Metcalf, who wants her to remain close to home at a more affordable college. The script is terrific. The movie is terrific. It will not make as much money or be seen by as many people as *Wonder Woman*, the DC Comics-based story of Amazonian warrior Diana, played by Gal Gadot, who leaves home and joins an American pilot in 20th Century Europe to fight with the Allies in World War I. But Greta Gerwig's screenplay for *Lady Bird* created a tremendous amount of buzz. It was nominated for an Oscar. It's added to the ongoing conversation that takes place in the movies. Greta Gerwig has written a bulletproof screenplay.

So a bulletproof idea can be an indie or a studio idea. The real difference can typically be found in the scale of the stories and the relative weight given to the three C's of the idea. Independent movies tend to lean more on character than concept. They're also less likely to capture the interest of buyers based on the idea alone, unless the buyer is already familiar with and interested in the writer. Character-driven ideas are generally referred to as "execution dependent." That may sound silly. Aren't all movies execution dependent? High concept and franchise-driven movies can be botched as easily as character-driven movies, can't they? Well, yes and no. If you turn your original screenplay in to Sony Pictures on the same weekend as the writer who's just finished penning the latest installment in the *Spiderman* franchise, the studio executives will not apply the same standards and criteria to the two scripts in deciding which gets made. They're making *Spiderman*. Even if it needs tons of additional script work at a cost of millions of dollars, they're making that movie. Whether or not they make your original screenplay is entirely discretionary. Your original script, whether character or concept driven, must hit the bulls-eye. It has to be bulletproof. Execution-dependent ideas are harder to sell and get made, independently and especially at studios, they require a screenplay that really packs a punch. Of course, if the spec you've written is *Get Out*, or *Moonlight*, or *Manchester by the Sea*, you have nothing to worry about.

Is This the Idea for Me?

So now you have your idea. You've vetted it and determined that it feels fresh, or at least promises a fresh approach. You understand where it sits on the landscape of studio and independent movies. So . . . is this the screenplay you should write? Probably, yes. But sometimes not. You have to ask yourself if this is an idea you can write effectively. Every writer is stronger in certain areas than others. Your idea won't be bulletproof, it really can't be, if you don't feel you're the best person to write it. Know your orientation and your skill set as a writer. Let that determine which ideas you choose to pursue, and which ones you hold off on, let go of entirely, or perhaps even pass along to others. We're not particularly inventive when it comes to conceiving action sequences. And generally speaking, we don't write action movies. If you've come up with a concept for a horror film, and you haven't seen a horror film since you were twelve, it's possible you should not be writing this idea, at least not in this way. Consider again the concept for *Groundhog Day*. That could have been developed as a horror film.* Perhaps you can spin your horror idea into a comedy or some other genre you're more comfortable writing. If not, you may have to hand it off to a friend who loves horror, or partner with someone who has a real passion for and command of the genre. Or you can try it yourself. Maybe you'll discover something about yourself and your writing you'd never have expected. You may even have something new to contribute to the genre as a relative outsider. In general, though, you're likely best off writing the kinds of movies you most like to watch. If you've never thought about that before, think about it now. It may save you an enormous amount of time as you work to define your creative voice and determine what you have to add to the conversation of the movies.

Think carefully about the movies you love most. Not "The Best" movies. Don't consult AFI's top 100 list. We all know *Citizen Kane*'s great and we all love *The Godfather,* Parts 1 and 2. We're talking about the movies you love, your favorites. Comedies, dramas, thrillers, action movies, horror movies, sci-fi... What are the movies that you can return to time after time without ever getting tired of them? The ones that come up when you're channel surfing and you simply can't help yourself from watching the rest, no matter where it is in the story, because you just love it that much? (Okay, go ahead and keep *The Godfather.*) Make the list. Pick five or ten. Twenty. It's actually a very good and helpful exercise in determining the kind of movie you're likely to enjoy working on and the kind you might, in fact, be best suited to write. Let these movies be your North Star in the genre you choose to pursue, in the quality you strive for, and in the general inspiration you find within them.

A final anecdote from the beginning of our own career to illustrate the process and importance of arriving at the bulletproof idea: In 1993,

---

*In fact, it was many years later, see 2017's *Happy Death Day,* written by Scott Lobdell, from Blumhouse Productions.

we wrote a screenplay called *People of Girth* about four frustrated, binge-eating customers who take over a 24 hour all-you-can-eat buffet and hold the manager hostage after he tries to kick them out. *People of Girth* turned some heads as an idea and as a completed screenplay, but the script was far from bulletproof. In fact, it was riddled with exactly the kinds of holes we're writing this book to help you avoid. We did not make a penny from *People of Girth*, but for all its shortcomings there were those who appreciated the potential of the concept and the comic voice of the script. It was a reasonably good writing sample.

A writing sample is a script that displays your talent in some fashion and can help to start a conversation with industry professionals — managers or agents or producers — even if the script you've written isn't "the one," even if it doesn't sell. So with *People of Girth,* we had what we hoped was a writing sample that might land us an agent. Those hopes, it turned out, were in vain. Mostly. We submitted the script to twenty different agents. All of the agents passed (including one who signed his generally complimentary rejection letter, "a lifelong member of Weight Watchers"). All but one, that is.

Jordan Bayer had recently left one of the big agencies and struck out on his own, establishing the boutique agency, Original Artists. He read *People of Girth* and asked if we wanted to meet for breakfast. Over a couple of smoked fish platters at the long since closed Stage Deli in Century City, Jordan told us he didn't think he could sell our script, but that we showed a fresh comic voice that was potentially more commercial than the script we'd written. He told us that if we really wanted, he could send *People of Girth* out to some producers and executives, and that maybe the writing sample would generate a few meetings. From those meetings, he continued, maybe an idea would emerge that we could then go and pitch, and that maybe, just maybe, we could find a studio to pay us Writers Guild minimum to write a script. But that was a real long shot and it was not the path Jordan was recommending. The path that Jordan was recommending was for us to start over from scratch with a more mainstream, commercial idea. A bulletproof idea.

He even offered to help us vet these ideas. He had no idea what he was getting himself into.

Two weeks later, determined to make the most of his offer and the opportunity, we were back at the Stage Deli, only this time we came prepared with sixteen original ideas. Sixteen! That's about eleven to thirteen more than anyone not married to you should reasonably be expected to listen to. But we were young and inexperienced, and more than a little over-eager. We'd finally found someone we believed could help jumpstart our career, and we weren't about to let him go until we'd road tested pretty much every idea we ever had. It wasn't until the very end, when all the lox and whitefish was gone from our plates and Jordan's weary eyes were beginning to glaze over, that we finally pitched a concept that caught his attention. It was about a slacker twelve year-old who becomes a genius magically overnight, upsetting the expectations of his friends, his family, and his teachers. This was 1993, when Macaulay Culkin was one of the biggest stars on the planet. There was an appetite at the studios for family comedies with younger leads — that is, a path to getting the movie made. Jordan thought there might be something there if we could just bring the fresh comic voice of *People of Girth* to this more studio-friendly idea. That's all we needed to hear.

We wrote two drafts of our child genius script and neither gained much traction with Jordan. After the first he gave us an extensive list of notes and questions to consider. We tried our best to implement those notes and respond to those questions. We treated them like we'd just been given the answers to the test, figuring that we simply could not fail if we just followed his instructions. We were wrong. There's an art to responding to notes just as there is to writing an original script, and we simply hadn't acquired the wisdom, experience, or tools yet to understand how best to incorporate his feedback.* After he read our second draft he called and delivered the bad news, "Guys," he said, "this may not be the one."

---

* More on responding to notes in Chapter Nine.

We were devastated. But something inside us — very possibly desperation — told us this *was* the one. We just hadn't done it right. So we packed our bags, jumped in the car, and drove to Vegas to figure out how and where we'd gone so wrong. We booked a room at the Sahara for fifteen bucks a night and headed for the Fashion Show Mall for a bite. We sat at the food court there, and we asked ourselves a simple question that cracked the entire process of writing our script open for us and planted the seed for the bulletproof approach we're sharing in this book.

This was a movie about a 12 year-old who becomes a genius magically. It was the kind of movie Disney might have made at the time, long before they acquired Marvel and LucasFilm and Pixar. So we asked ourselves, *"If Disney were making our movie, what would it look like?"* For the first time, we looked at our idea from the top down, from the studio's perspective, and when we did that the answers came so quickly and clearly it was as if the heavens had opened and the angels were singing. We could barely write the ideas for our characters and the steps of our story down fast enough. Not because we'd discovered some kind of secret formula. There is no formula. But because, for the first time, we could see a structure and a tone that would result in a movie that a studio with a particular brand might release, that they could market to the public, and that people might get excited about and come to see with their families. The creative decisions, the story choices, of which there are hundreds in every script, weren't just about us anymore, and what we might find funny, or scary, or clever. They were also about our future partner, the studio. They were about what movies actually look like when you see the finished product in the theater. By the end of our lunch, bursting with confidence and enthusiasm, we sent Jordan a postcard with the message that we'd cracked the idea and he'd be hearing from us again in a few weeks time.

A few weeks later we emerged, as promised, with a new draft for Jordan to read. He was finally able to see the concept he'd first heard at the Stage Deli born out in the manner he'd imagined. And though there was still some rewriting to do, the work going forward was different. We weren't feeling around in the dark, getting carried away with ideas we'd come to almost arbitrarily. We understood what kind of movie this was, who it was for — what kind of buyer and what kind of audience. We'd endured a few massive wrong turns and a painfully steep learning curve to get there. But with a good amount of determination and persistence on our part, and patience on Jordan's, we finally emerged in the spring of 1994 with a script for a coming-of-age comedy called *The Whiz Kid*. Within four days of reading our official submission draft, Jordan got a young Elijah Wood attached to star and sold the script to 20th Century Fox as part of a two-picture deal worth almost $750,000, significantly more than Writers Guild minimum. After five years of trying, we'd finally sold a movie to a major studio. Our career was launched. But it wasn't that studio offer that marked the launch. It was the shift in perspective and approach that took place at the food court of the Fashion Show Mall in Vegas. It was the question, *How would Disney do it*? that encapsulated the simultaneous bottom-up and top-down approach to screenwriting we've applied ever since. That is the essence of the bulletproof process that has served us throughout our career and which guides the work we're going to do with you going forward.

finding bulletproof models

If you were raising a child, you might identify certain attributes you'd like to cultivate within that child — kindness, generosity, humility, courage, self-confidence, etc. You'd look to people in your life, family members, community members, people you know about but whom you may never have met, who exemplify these qualities. You'd learn what you could from these people and you'd use them as examples as you raise and guide your child. These people are models for the kind of person you hope your child will become, or at least for some of the qualities you hope they'll grow to possess. You're not encouraging your child to be someone they're not. You want them to be unique in the world, while also learning and internalizing all the valuable lessons there are to learn from those who've come before.

So, too, in the movies. You're not creating and writing in a vacuum. Some aspects of what you're trying to do with your screenplay have been done by others, perhaps with great success. You want to learn from these writers and from their movies. You want to benefit as much as possible from the successes and the failures of those who've come before and the movie models they've provided for you.

By now you have an idea you're passionate about. You've got your concept, your character, and your context. You know the genre you're writing in. You've talked about it with people whose opinions you trust and respect, and you're feeling pretty good, confident that if you execute this idea well, this spec could mark the beginning of your career. That's a great feeling. Embrace it. Enjoy it. At some point not too long from now the work is going to get harder, and that confidence and enthusiasm may be more difficult to maintain. But we're not there yet. This is the fun part. In fact, this may be the most fun you'll have at work until you actually sell your script. This is the part where you get to watch lots of movies — the models for the script you're about to write. Familiarizing yourself with, and analyzing, the models for your screenplay will help illuminate the path your story needs to follow and expose mistakes and blind alleys for you to avoid. It's also a critical step in writing a bulletproof screenplay.

Again, your goal is a script that gets talked about, that attracts buzz. How do you achieve that? How do you attract the kind of attention and conversation that gets your script noticed and passed from one stakeholder to the next in the Hollywood chain? By adding something to your genre, by doing something in a way it hasn't been done before. Think about *The Hangover* in comedy. *Deadpool* in the superhero genre. *Get Out* in horror. You cannot add to the creative conversation that takes place in and around the movies unless you're familiar with the movies that have framed and shaped that conversation thus far. Literacy counts. In fact, it's essential. The good news is, we're not talking about *real* literacy. You don't have to go out and read *Beowulf* or *Middlemarch*. This is *movie* literacy — the kind that makes your parents or your spouse roll their eyes when you tell them you're "working," or "doing research." You just have to watch *Home Alone, Inception, The Shawshank Redemption . . .* iconic movies from your genre that help frame the creative conversation you aspire to be a part of.

Taking Your Place at the Table

Of course, finding the right models for your movie is not just about attracting buzz and being film literate. It's also about writing the best script you can write, being the best writer you can be. Think about your idea. Who are the master screenwriters of your genre? We started out in the mid-90s writing concept and character-driven comedies that aimed to be funny, thematically rich, and emotionally satisfying. The writers whose movies we looked to probably more than anyone else's were Lowell Ganz & Babaloo Mandel (*Night Shift, Splash, City Slickers, Parenthood*). What are the iconic movies that are the antecedents to the script you're writing? Imagine a table with the writers, directors and producers who've made the biggest contribution to your genre sitting around it. Who's at that table? What are the movies that earned them a seat? You need to know these movies inside and out before there's a seat there for you.

When we were developing *The Family Man*, our production executive, Jon Shestack, gave us a very specific and inspiring charge. He told us he wanted our movie to be the one future filmmakers would look to as they craft similar stories of their own. Years later, we were told that executives at Disney Animation had referenced *The Family Man* as a model in story meetings. You want your movie on the list others will someday look to and talk about. You want a seat at that table. You want to become the model. Set the bar high and learn from the best.

To be clear and to reiterate, this is not about trying to discern a formula for you to follow in the writing of your own script. There are no formulas. It's not about *copying* movies that have come before. It's about learning from them, understanding better the language of your own movie. Learning from your predecessors does not make you any less of an original talent. Guillermo del Toro and Wes Anderson draw inspiration and lessons from other filmmaker's movies, too! Don't try to reinvent the wheel from scratch. You don't score points for originality just for originality's sake. You score points for what works. And what works, what has always worked, is original work that shows respect for dramatic and genre conventions and builds on what's come before.

So consider your idea, and now think about comparable movies that have some similarities to what you're trying to do conceptually, that use a similar character as a protagonist. Start making a list. You're going to be watching these movies. If you've seen them before, you're going to be watching them again. They will look different to you now that you're trying to write something in the same genre, or with a similar character, device, or story engine. List the great movies and the bad movies; you can learn from all of them. But take special note of the good ones, the ones that get it right. Go first to the iconic. Do this for the obvious reason that you want to learn from the best, but do it also for the opportunity it provides to clear the highest bar and overcome the most challenging obstacles standing between where you are now and where you aspire to be. To earn a seat at the table.

Watching with a Discerning Eye

Once you have your list of the movies that have gotten it right and the ones that have gone slightly or even horribly awry, start watching. Take notes. Pay attention to what works and what doesn't work. What's the structure? Is the movie too plot-heavy and confusing? Is it simple and elegant? How does the writer establish the lead character? How does the movie open? How many set pieces are there and how do they function in the story? Are there multiple storylines? If so, how do they connect, how are they integrated? Are you writing a sci-fi adventure script?

Compare *Star Wars: A New Hope* and *Star Wars: The Last Jedi*. What do you notice about the way each of these movies attempts to draw us into the story, and the way the various characters and plot lines are developed and tied together? Which did this more effectively, and why? Are you writing a family comedy? Take a look at *Daddy's Home* and compare it with our movie *Old Dogs*. We love *Old Dogs* and it's tremendously satisfying when kids who grew up watching the movie quote lines back to us. But *Daddy's Home* is a more fully realized movie. And it was more commercially successful; it spawned a sequel. Why? What's the difference? Take a look at the John Hughes family comedies. Watch *Uncle Buck*.

The day we arrived in Vegas and headed to the Fashion Show Mall to figure out where we'd gone wrong on our first two drafts of *The Whiz Kid*, the essence of our epiphany was that we hadn't chosen the right models for our movie. If we had just asked ourselves *"How would Disney do it?"* at the very beginning, instead of beating our heads against the wall trying to come up with any and every possible consequence of our protagonist's granted wish, we might have saved ourselves months of work and anguish, not to mention the time of the agent who was helping guide us. We were a wish fulfillment comedy about a twelve year-old who magically becomes a genius. What's the model? *Big*. That's the movie, right? Not the movie we want to *copy*, the movie we want to learn from, to use as our bar, our North Star.

In or around the year *Big* was released there were two other adult/child body-switching comedies released — *Like Father, Like Son*, starring Dudley Moore and Kirk Cameron, and *Vice Versa*, with Judge Reinhold and Fred Savage. Of the three, *Big* was the critical and fan favorite, and the only one to garner Academy Award nominations for its writers and star, Gary Ross and Anne Spielberg, and Tom Hanks. It wasn't just a commercially successful movie, it was a really good movie, funny and poignant. *Big* was at the time, and may well remain today, the best of its genre. What better model for *The Whiz Kid*, and for us as writers, than *Big*?

25

Of course, there were other models. What about *Rookie of the Year*? Not a film you're likely to find on AFI's top 100. You might not even remember it, or ever have heard of it. But *Rookie of the Year*, released in 1995, was about a 12 year-old baseball lover whose broken arm heals in a way that allows him to pitch over 100 miles per hour, earning him a spot on the Cubs pitching roster. A coming-of-age fantasy fulfillment story, like ours. It had just come out at the time we were writing *The Whiz Kid* and it had done very well for its studio, Twentieth Century Fox. *Rookie of the Year* was on our list of models, once we finally figured out what kind of movie we were writing, along with pretty much every other coming-of-age fantasy fulfillment comedy we could come up with. Now, *The Whiz Kid* was not produced. It has not become, like *Big*, the movie others point to if they're interested in writing in this genre. But it did launch our career, it was our first big spec sale. And guess who bought it? Twentieth Century Fox . . . for Bob Harper, producer of *Rookie of the Year*! Finding the right models is essential, practical, and, if our own career is any indication, effective.

Finding Inspiration and Information in Those Who've Come Before

When we were writing *The Family Man*, we spent a good bit of time talking about *Groundhog Day, Peggy Sue Got Married, Heaven Can Wait,* and *It's a Wonderful Life* — movies about characters who have an opportunity to see their lives from a different perspective, how it might have turned out under other circumstances. We also talked about the less distinguished Jim Belushi vehicle *Mr. Destiny,* about an adult character who attributes all the problems in his life to having missed the "big catch" in a high school championship game. He then gets to see what his life would have looked like had he made that catch. None of these movies was our movie precisely, but they all explored similar themes or shared a similar conceit, and they all provided instruction and inspiration, goals to shoot for and pitfalls to avoid.

The models you choose now will be useful to you throughout the process of writing your script, and after. As you discover more and more about your story and your characters, and the conventions of your genre, you may add to your list of movies to watch for instruction and return to others you've already looked at. When you sell your movie, and sit down with studio executives for the first time to get script notes and talk about the way forward, some of these models may find their way into the conversation, and new ones may be introduced.

We'll never forget the first studio meeting we had at Paramount Pictures when producer Mark Gordon brought our script *Guam Goes to the Moon* over with him from Fox. Our new studio executive was Paramount V.P. of Production Don Granger. The reason we'll never forget this meeting, which took place over twenty years ago, is that Don Granger gave us perhaps the best and most inspiring script notes we've ever received. What was so great about his notes? First, he had a copy of our script on his lap with a few lines scribbled on the cover, but he never actually opened our script, nor did he consult a memo put together for him by a junior creative executive at the company. He was, at least for this first meeting, focused solely on the big picture. Don Granger understood the movie *Guam Goes to the Moon* wanted to be. Before he said a word about our screenplay or what he thought we needed to change and why, he talked with us about the tradition of movies like *Guam* that inspired him and contributed to his interest in being in this business. He mentioned classic films like *The Guns of Navarone* and drew us into an enthusiastic conversation, a movie lover's conversation, about the relative merits of *Navarone*, *A Bridge Too Far* and *Bridge on the River Kwai*. Only then did he turn to the business at hand and say, "Okay, now let's talk about Guam." He then identified four areas that he believed were critically important to our movie and how there were opportunities for us to mine these areas further and come up with something more impactful. Once he knew that we understood the difference between where we were and where we all wanted to be, the meeting was over. That was it. No line notes, no scene notes, no character notes, except as they related to the big idea of our movie — the character (or, in this case, ensemble of characters), the concept, and the context. When we finished our rewrite, the studio hired a director and began the campaign to make the movie.

As in life, so too in the movies — models are important. They're important in the embryonic stage, when you're still defining your idea and establishing your dreams and visions for what it might become, they're important while you're writing, looking for direction within your structure and within individual scenes, and they're important when you're revising and refining, moving ever closer to the great movie your screenplay yearns to be.

Now go have the most fun you'll ever have doing homework. Make your list of models and start watching!

chapter three
———————

the bulletproof "one-pager"

Here's what's going to happen a few months from now when you've completed a submission draft of your screenplay and you're ready to turn it in to a manager, agent, or producer: They're going to give it to someone to read and evaluate it for them. That may seem ridiculous to you. *How hard is it to read a hundred-page screenplay?! This is everything that's wrong with Hollywood! No wonder movies are so awful; no one reads the scripts!* You can add this outrage to your list of things to get over as you navigate your way to success. Managers, agents, and executives have assistants, interns, and freelance script readers evaluate screenplays because there simply and literally isn't enough time in the day for them to read all of the scripts that are submitted to them while also servicing their clients and their current projects in development and production. Reading scripts is not hard, but it is time consuming. Talking with writers and offering feedback, giving notes, is time consuming. And most of these writers come back for a second bite at the apple with a rewrite of their script for consideration, just as we did all those years ago with Jordan Bayer. It's all part of the job for anyone to whom you'd be submitting your script, but you are not the only one asking them to do that part of their job. You're not the only writer in town. And you're certainly not the only writer trying to break in. If you're going to get the attention of that agent or manager or production executive, you're first going to have to be able to survive the reader who evaluates material for them. The reader is their first line of defense against the swarm of writers trying to break in. Your goal is to penetrate that line of defense. We're going to try to help you do that with this next step in the development of your screenplay. The Bulletproof One-Pager.

When the reader evaluates your script they'll include a one-page synopsis of your story. That synopsis will — or at least it should — support their determination as to whether or not your screenplay warrants further consideration. If the recommendation is PASS, it's unlikely whoever ordered the evaluation will ever bother to read the synopsis, let alone the entire script. If it's RECOMMEND or CONSIDER, the person who requested the read will take a look at the reader's logline, and perhaps the synopsis, and decide for him or herself whether it's worth their own time to read it. One of the main objectives of the one-pager is for you to do as much of that reader's job for them as you can, in the way you want it done. You can't actually write their synopsis for them, but you can make damn sure that the script you've submitted holds up and provides a fabulous opportunity for them to showcase your story with a simple, clear, and compelling one-page synopsis. Most of these readers are experienced and skilled at doing justice to a good story when they find one. Many are writers themselves, and they genuinely prefer reading good scripts to bad ones. Plus, when they find a real winner, they're a hero. Making that reader a hero is all part of your mission.

All that said, penetrating the executive's first line of defense is really the secondary benefit of, and purpose behind, the bulletproof one-pager. The primary objective here is to provide you, the writer, with a roadmap that will help guide you from this point forward in the process of breaking your story and writing your script. See that? Everybody wins!

Now, before you set out to write your one pager, there are still a few things you need to know. And they're really important. Proceed without them at your peril. First, you need a basic grasp of story structure. Second, you need to know both what your movie is about, and what your movie is *really* about. And third, you need to develop a vision of how your story is going to play out over the course of a hundred and five minutes. (*Do they really need to be any longer? Really, do they . . . ?!*)

A Basic Grasp of Story Structure

We're not the first screenwriting book to go down this road and it's quite possible, likely even, that by the time you arrive at this extended cup of coffee with us you've already taken in the lessons of structure gurus like Syd Field or Robert McKee, or Googled "How to Write a Screenplay," any of which will do just fine. Tons of ink has been spilled on the topic of screenplay structure and lots of money has been spent on books, courses, and seminars. The truth is, not much has changed since Aristotle first explored what makes stories work in his *Poetics*, circa 335 BCE. Stories have a beginning, middle, and end. Three acts. The first is the set up, the second introduces and develops the implications and complications, the third is the resolution. Unless you're a fan of avant-garde cinema, every movie you have ever seen that has been distributed in theaters, on television, or streamed online has three acts. So will your screenplay, or you will not sell it. That's clear, right? It doesn't matter if you're writing a studio movie or an indie. Your screenplay will adhere to the three-act structure, or you will not sell it. If there are any skeptics, cynics or artistic purists remaining among you who simply refuse to believe you need to buy into this system and adhere to a convention of storytelling that dates back thousands of years, consider the following analogy: Imagine you're buying a house. The house is beautiful and distinctive, a real showpiece. But once you enter you realize it has no bathrooms or closets and the kitchen is on the roof. Would you still buy it? There are all sorts of creative liberties you can take and freedoms you can express in designing and building a house. But certain basic expectations and structural conventions must be met for that house to be reasonably considered inhabitable. Your screenplay is a blueprint for a movie. It will have three acts. *Capiche*?

Your first act will introduce us to the world in which your story takes place. It will introduce your main characters and serve as the set up for your concept. The context, the character(s), the concept. Your first act is the dramatic expression of your movie idea — this person, in that situation, under these circumstances — and everything we need to know to be engaged in the journey to come. End Act One.

Your second act is essentially the proof of the dramatic viability and potential of your idea. We'll see the impact of your concept on your characters and the world they inhabit — that could be hilarious if you're a comedy, scary if you're a thriller or a horror movie, magical if you're a fantasy adventure story. The dramatic stakes will be raised as your story progresses. Your characters will be repeatedly and increasingly challenged, prodded to become the people your movie is inviting them to be. (Note: if no one in your movie is tested and defined further as a character as a result of what they've been through in your story, then what was the point of putting them, or us, through the journey in the first place? But more on this in a moment.) Most important of all, your second act will be absorbing, captivating, *entertaining* . . . it will take us to another place, immerse us in the lives of others, in places we have never been. At the end of your second act, your lead character or ensemble will appear hopelessly distant from their goal as expressed by or for them at the end of your first act. They are significantly worse off than when we met them. It will appear that they have failed. End Act Two.

As your story turns into act three, your character(s) will have the opportunity to call upon their experience and lessons learned in act two. They may emerge with greater resolve than ever before, bringing all their resources to bear in order to solve the problem you've placed before them. Or they may fail, revealing some deeper truth about them, the challenges they face, and the world around them. In the end, they may win or they may lose. That will have everything to do with the tone of your script and the message you intend to convey through your story. One way or another, there is resolution.

If your screenplay is successful, truly bulletproof, your reader (and the audience that ultimately leaves the theater after watching your movie) will actually feel something akin to what your characters are feeling following the third act resolution of your story. Justice has been served! Love has conquered fear! Good has defeated evil! Truth has won out! Or . . . the outcome may not be nearly as positive and uplifting, but it reveals some truth about your character, about us and the world we live in in a way that is poignant, heartbreaking, beautiful. Either way, when your third act delivers on the potential of the two that preceded it, and your reader feels that, the rewards are tangible, something to shoot for every time.

What Your Movie's About vs. What Your Movie's *Really* About

Now that you're fleshing out your story, it's time to take the question of what your movie's about to the next level. If a friend or relative asks you what you're working on, you tell them your idea, just like we discussed in Chapter One. "I'm writing a script about a disgraced and disgruntled Confederate soldier who hijacks the Lincoln funeral train in an effort to reignite the Civil War, and the three Union misfits who are hired to recover the train and bring him to justice."* Cool! But one question you'll be forced to confront as you develop this idea further is, what's the point? We get the idea, but what's this movie really about?

Every movie is a debate among competing values, perspectives, and beliefs expressed through characters and story. Does love triumph over hate or fear? Is the quest for truth and justice more powerful than greed and corruption? Lajos Egri writes compellingly about this in the opening to his *The Art of Dramatic Writing*. His vocabulary and method may differ from other's, including ours. He refers to the proposition, the argument a dramatic story puts forward as its premise, where we might call it the theme. Potato, po-tah-to. The point is, every story worth telling, and worth spending two hours and your hard-earned dollars on, should have a point. What's yours? This is the time to think about it and develop it as you craft the story of your movie. A screenwriter is like a trial lawyer making a case to a jury. What's your argument and how are you going to go about advancing and proving it over 105 pages? The point of your movie is waiting for you, hidden within your idea if you don't already know it. You just need to tease it out so that you can build the best and most impactful case for what your movie is *really* about over the course of your three acts.

How Your Story Will Play Out

Okay, so you have your idea. You've taken in the models and seen how masters and hacks alike have executed movies that tackle similar subject matter, themes, characters, or share your genre or other aspects of the script you plan to write. You feel excited, confident, like you get what you have to do. You also know what your movie's about — not just your plot, what happens to whom, but thematically. You know what you're trying to say with your story and your characters as your

---

* This is a shameless plug for *Union Flyer*, an original idea we've always loved.

subtle messengers. You may feel like you're ready to write. Please don't. That would be a massive mistake, at least as far as your screenplay is concerned. Trust us that a little time and thought invested now will save you an enormous amount of time and potential anguish later.

The time you need now is for imagining the way your story should play out in its broadest strokes. What would the Warner Bros. or the Fox Searchlight version of your idea look like? Think about your characters and your device. Think about what you're trying to say in your movie, what's inspired you to write it, what you genuinely believe to be true as far as this story is concerned. Think about how to make a dramatic case for all of that. What would have to happen? Take notes. Don't be rigid, be bold. Be willing to go off on some tangents — better now than later, when you're actually writing your script! Revisit your models. What have they taught you about what works and what doesn't work? You can make notes for scenes and dialogue if you're so inspired, but don't use them yet, not in your one-pager — you don't begin a blueprint for a house by picking out the bathroom tile. Fashion your story, just in the most general terms for now. Go ahead, we'll leave you alone for a bit. Then come back when you're done and we're going to go about telling your entire story on one page . . . like the reader evaluating your screenplay is eventually going to do.

The Story of Your Movie on One Page

If you've vetted your idea properly and sufficiently, consulted the models, and explored the dramatic and thematic arcs of the story you'd like to tell, you should be able to lay it all out in broad strokes in a single page. Again, the benefits of telling your story on a single page are twofold: it's precisely the space your script reader will be devoting to their synopsis, and it will keep you honest, focused, and directed as you continue to flesh out your characters and your plot. It will allow you to maintain a 30,000 foot view of your story at the same time that you're toiling with every character and plot detail. It will keep you from getting lost in the weeds.

In developing our own ideas, or working on jobs, we generally try to hit nine marks in one page. This expands to many, many more as we advance in our process toward an outline, but the one-pager — the first schematic of our movie idea laid out from start to finish — shapes up like this:

1. We begin by setting up our character and where he or she sits in the world. Succinctly.

2. We introduce the opportunity or challenge, what some call the "inciting incident," or the "call to adventure," that sets the story in motion.

3. Next is the first act break where the character commits to and sets out on a journey — could be dramatic, could be comedic — that will change them and their world irrevocably.

4. On or around page 45 we introduce a turn that injects game-changing new information or circumstances and significantly ups the challenge and the stakes in the story.

5. Then we have our mid-act reversal, which is just what it sounds like. It's a bigger, more significant and unexpected change of circumstances that forces our character to regroup and possibly change course. If we're a fantasy fulfillment story, this is where things begin to go awry. If it's a "be careful what you wish for" story, this is where the character may finally figure out how to turn what initially seemed like a curse to his or her advantage.

6. Around page 75 we shake things up again with a late second act twist or escalation before . . .

7. The end of Act Two. Whether your second act began on a total high or a descent into darkness, this is where all seems lost. The end of your second act is the worst possible outcome of the circumstances you introduced in your concept. It can't get any worse than this.

8. And then it does. In our third act, before we resolve our story, we put our characters through one final test and give them an opportunity to rise above their circumstances and prove themselves.

9. This opportunity generally comes in the form of a final confrontation or set-piece in which our lead has to dig deep and call upon qualities and talents he or she may never have known they possessed. They finally realize who they are, what's most important to them, and how they can bring all their resources to bear to make their world as it is more as they believe it can and should be. *Finis*.

Now let's take a look at what a one-pager might actually look like in practice. See if the broad strokes of this movie are at all familiar, and if the main turns of the story can be captured successfully in a single page . . .

STAR WARS*

1. Aspiring pilot LUKE SKYWALKER is stuck working on his aunt and uncle's farm when all he really wants is to join his friends at the Academy, training to join the Rebellion in their struggle against the evil Empire and its dark leader, DARTH VADER.

2. Luke discovers a message from Rebellion leader PRINCESS LEIA hidden within a droid his uncle has purchased, calling for help from Jedi Master OBI-WAN KENOBE.

3. The recluse Obi-Wan urges Luke to join him on his quest to deliver the information within the droid to the Rebellion. Luke resists, but when he returns home to discover his aunt and uncle murdered by Empire Storm Troopers, he realizes he has no one now but mentor Obi-Wan, and nowhere to turn but the Rebellion.

4. Luke and Obi-Wan recruit maverick, mercenary pilot HAN SOLO to deliver them to the planet Alderaan, per Leia's instructions . . . for a price. Obi-Wan begins training Luke in the ways of The Force during this journey. But when they arrive in the Alderaan system, they discover the planet's been destroyed by the Empire's most powerful weapon, the Death Star.

5. Their ship is drawn inside the Death Star via tractor beam, their presence — especially Obi-Wan's — sensed by DARTH VADER, whose mission is to wipe out

---

* These "One-Pagers" appear here across two-pages for formatting reasons and for the purpose of illustration only. That said, don't get so stuck on the length of your One-Pager that you lose sight of the larger principle and purpose — keep it basic and succinct, telling the broad strokes of your story on a single page, more or less. If you're slightly under or over it does not invalidate the step or diminish the potential of your story.

the rebellion and all remaining Jedi, including his former master, Obi-Wan. Trying to avoid detection and capture, Luke and co. discover Princess Leia is being held prisoner on the Death Star and she's currently scheduled for execution. What began as a "deliver the package" mission is now a rescue mission, with their lives, Leia's, and the fate of the entire Rebellion at stake.

6. While Luke and his team secure the Princess's release, Obi-Wan sets out to disarm the tractor beam that holds their ship captive on the Death Star. In his effort to secure their safe escape, Obi-Wan sacrifices his own life, distracting the storm troopers and allowing himself to be cut down by Vader.

7. Luke is devastated, but Leia and the plans for the Death Star are successfully delivered to the rebel base. Now that he has his reward money, Han begs off the mission to destroy the Death Star, but the Empire has tracked Han's ship and now knows the location of the rebel base and is prepared to destroy it in a matter of minutes.

8. As Rebel fighters attack the Death Star in an effort to deliver a fatal blow, the Death Star's guns and Empire Storm Troopers pick off the Rebel Fighters one by one. Vader himself is on Luke's tail. He's about to blow Luke, the last remaining rebel threat to the Death Star, away when Han swoops in at the last second, firing on Vader and his wingmen and leaving Luke a clear path to take his shot.

9. Luke destroys the Death Star as Vader caroms alone off into space. Luke and Han are celebrated as heroes by Leia and the entire Rebellion.

Of course there's so much more magic and wonder to *Star Wars* than just these nine steps in a one-pager. But the basic foundation of the story, and even much of what you need to know of its characters, is there.

Here's the thing: We typically have nine steps. Blake Snyder has fifteen. Syd Field, Robert McKee, and all the others probably have their own number. We can't all be right! The point is to adhere to a basic, proven structure for storytelling. Try not to get too religious about the way any one expert, real or self-proclaimed, tells you it must be done. It's true that all great stories can be broken into three acts. But not all stories that are broken into three acts are great. The same holds true of the one-pager. You should be able to fit the broad strokes of your story, its basic structural beats, on a single page. But fitting all the major turns of your story on one page does not necessarily mean you have a bullet-proof story. It's not any particular "system" that makes your screenplay bulletproof; it's a general respect for the form combined with a healthy dose of inspiration, originality, creativity, and strategic, thoughtful planning.

Your one-pager provides a perfect opportunity to return to the people you know and trust to help vet your ideas. Talk them through your story. If it's laid out in one page it shouldn't take more than just a few minutes. Are they with you? Are they excited? If so, great; you're ready to proceed to Chapter Four and drill down deeper. If they're not, you have to take that seriously and think about what it means. If the people who are rooting most enthusiastically for you to succeed are having trouble making heads or tails of even the basic, broad strokes of your story, how do you expect to fare any better with some anonymous script reader who may have gotten up on the wrong side of the bed with a dozen other scripts to read by folks they don't know and aren't personally invested in? You have to return to your idea, as we did so many years ago with *The Whiz Kid* (and have done many times since), and go on a bit of a treasure hunt, searching for the movie your idea is yearning to become. The message of our story in *The Whiz Kid* was that there are no shortcuts in life. Success has to be earned. It's the same in the writing of the bulletproof screenplay. No skipping steps. Get your one-pager right. Make the basic foundation of your story rock solid. Do that, and you will be well on your way to raising eyebrows all over town.

Here's another example of a one-pager, this one from our own files. The project is called *The Minutemen*, and the one-pager and script that emerged from it served us well, really better than we ever could have reasonably expected...

THE MINUTEMEN

1. Theoretical physicist VIRGIL ST. CLAIRE and his lifelong friends and Dept. of Defense lab partners MARTY and ZEKE believe they've finally delivered on their childhood dream of changing the world when they successfully test a device that allows them to travel back in time — though only for a matter of minutes and only within the past six months.

2. Exploiting Virgil's insatiable desire for recognition, acclaim, and female companionship, the team's DOD nemesis BARRY LEMMONS sets him up, using a female FBI agent who busts Virgil for revealing classified information in an effort to seduce her. The team is fired.

3. Marty and Zeke are furious at Virgil for costing them their jobs and their reputations. Then, Virgil's struck by inspiration and offers a solution to all their problems — use their scientific breakthrough to go into business for themselves as "freelance problem solvers," going back in time to correct costly mistakes in the lives of clients who will pay handsomely for the service.

4. The team's first client prospect is tech billionaire CLIVE VAN ETAN, who stands to lose half his fortune in a divorce due to an illicit tryst in an Atlantic City hotel. Van Etan balks at Virgil's offer of help. But when the self-dubbed "Minutemen," land in the news for their role in restoring $5,000 to a poor robbery victim, Van Etan comes calling . . . with a $1 million offer.

5. The Minutemen successfully intervene in the Van Etan affair, and others. Now they're on a roll, earning all the acclaim (and money) Virgil and Co.

could ever have desired. Virgil even finds a promising relationship with science reporter SUSAN COLLINS, with whom, in a touching romantic moment, he shares the time travel secret at the heart of their success.

6. Susan then shocks Virgil, betraying his trust by outing the Minutemen and their time travel secret on the front page of the New York Times, devastating Virgil and confirming Barry Lemmon's suspicions that The Minutemen have been exploiting DOD proprietary science and technology for their own personal benefit.

7. Once again out of work, and now in serious legal trouble, the friendship among Virgil, Zeke, and Marty is frayed seemingly beyond repair. But there's a bigger problem . . .

8. In the time since the DOD closed the Minutemen down, Lemmons has been using their tech for Defense Dept. covert operations. On their most recent mission they failed to close a sinkhole, which now threatens to grow quickly into a full scale black hole threatening the entire world. The DOD needs the minds and experience of The Minutemen to help close that hole.

9. Virgil gets the team back together for one last mission — going back in time to close the sinkhole from the other side, though it comes with the risk that they may not be able to return to the present. Together again, they save the world in a selfless and heroic act, and find themselves living in 1977 . . . where they just happen to know who wins the Super Bowl, the Kentucky Derby, etc. They're living high in the permissive 70s, their friendship and wealth restored.

What do we know from this one-pager?

We know — or at least can infer — that the only thing more important to Virgil than recognition is his friendships with Marty and Zeke. They've been friends since childhood. They shared a dream to change the world. That's powerful stuff. It also puts us, the audience, firmly in their corner. Yes, Virgil may have some self-serving tendencies and a weakness for the ladies, but at the end of the day he's a good friend and he really does want to use the gifts of his powerful intellect for the benefit of mankind. His friends, too. So we're rooting for them. And we intuitively dislike and distrust their antagonist, bureaucrat Barry Lemmons (whose name just begs us to hate him). Lemmons is manipulative and self-serving from the beginning, deliberately exploiting Virgil's Achilles heel to undermine a smarter, more talented and accomplished scientist. It's satisfying to finally see Lemmons bested and Virgil and his friends rewarded for their talent, ingenuity, and entrepreneurial spirit. These are things we want to believe in.

We know also that, in the end, The Minutemen's innate talent and ability, and their lifelong desire to make a difference in the world, wins out over Lemmon's selfish ambition and petty, competitive nature. And we know, perhaps even more powerfully, that the friendship among these three, and doing what's right, means more to them than life itself, as they're willing to risk all in coming together one last time for a mission that could cost them their lives even as it promises to save the world.

Finally, we know how our three acts are going to play out, and what and where the escalations and turns are. We have our structure. Filling in the blanks is no small task, but it's a helluva lot easier to do with this template, this map to help guide us going forward.

It should come as no surprise that our primary model for *The Minutemen* was Ivan Reitman's *Ghostbusters*, written by Dan Aykroyd and Harold Ramis. *Ghostbusters*, certainly in the early part of our career, probably impacted and influenced us more than any other movie. Ganz & Mandell's *Night Shift*, another favorite, directed by Ron Howard, also provided an inspiring model in tone, structure, and character, with our Virgil St. Claire owing no small debt to Michael Keaton's Bill Blazejowski. We sold *The Minutemen* as a pitch to *Family Man* producer Marc Abraham. When we submitted the script, Marc sensed it wasn't the kind of movie his company was likely to make. Because of the professional relationship and mutual respect that had developed between us over the years, he gave us a choice. He could give us notes on the script on the off chance it might evolve into something more aligned with the company's interests. Or we could have the project back to shop to other buyers more likely to make it. We chose the second option, and found a new home for the project at Disney, where executives wanted to make the movie as a teen comedy based on the story, characters, and tone of our script.

Meanwhile, *Ghostbusters* producer and director Ivan Reitman read *The Minutemen* and asked us to rewrite a sci-fi action script he'd optioned called *Evolution* as a comedy. We adapted *Evolution* for Ivan's company and within a year the project was set up at Dreamworks with a cast, a start date, and Ivan himself directing. Based on those results and the almost familial atmosphere that developed around that collaboration, Ivan engaged us to rewrite a second project for him, this one a mixed live-action animated musical originally written by the legendary William Goldman.

Meanwhile, time passed, years even, and nothing happened with *The Minutemen*, until . . .

We got a call out of the blue from our agent telling us that Andrew Gunn and Ann Marie Sanderlin, the Disney producers on *The Minutemen,* had slipped the script to the Disney Channel, which wanted to produce it as a Disney Channel original movie. At the time, we each had young children who loved the Disney Channel. *High School Musical* was playing in our houses practically 24/7. And after years of inactivity, this was an opportunity to see the movie made, which is, after all, why we write. For us, the decision was a no-brainer.

Now, *Minutemen* was a big hit for the channel*, but it was no *Ghostbusters*, and frankly, neither was *Evolution*. That's one reason this book isn't called *How to Win an Oscar,* or *How to Write a Blockbuster*. Because you, the writer, cannot control whether your movie wins awards or makes boatloads of money. All you can do is deliver the best version of your idea that you can, keeping in mind the various stakeholders who have to say yes in order for your script to get made.

In the end, our original pitch for *The Minutemen* yielded three jobs and two produced credits, *Evolution* in 2001 and *Minutemen* in 2007. For us, that *Minutemen* one-pager was 100% certified bulletproof. It takes some time and a considerable amount of thought, but a solid one-pager can prove enormously helpful and valuable. And it's just one page. If you're looking for homework, an exercise that might generate unexpected but significant benefits, return to your models. See how their stories lay out on a page. Now come back to your own original idea with fresh eyes and clear purpose and write your own bulletproof one-pager ... !

* "Disney's 'Minutemen' a ratings champ" by John Dempsey, *Daily Variety* January 28, 2008

building bulletproof characters

The greatest story and the bestselling book of all time begins with the creation of the world. We're talking about the bible of course. Take a look. God creates the heavens and the earth, the sun, moon and stars, the seas and dry land, fruit bearing trees, living creatures — fowl, fish and cattle, creepy crawly animals and insects. He creates the divisions between night and day and the rules that govern the physical world from the beginning of time to today. And then, as His final act before resting, He populates the world He's created. God literally fills the world with a cast of characters — first, Adam and Eve, then Cain and Abel, then Noah and his children. By the eleventh chapter of the book of Genesis, and the famous story of the Tower of Babel, the world is already so filled with people that we are spread across the face of the

Earth speaking multiple languages. These biblical characters who've become part of the collective consciousness of people the world over, their stories handed down from one generation to the next, are hardly a random act of creation. They are the point of creation. After all, what ultimate purpose can the biblical story serve without people to deliver its message? You, the screenwriter, are creating a much smaller world, but it must be a complete world nonetheless, populated with characters who serve your story and deliver your message.

By this time, you probably have a pretty good idea who the essential players populating your story are. You have a protagonist and perhaps an antagonist, and some supporting characters necessary to tell the broad strokes of your story and produce your one-pager. The question is, are they bulletproof? Because you want your characters to serve your story in the best and most creatively compelling and satisfying way possible. And you are also going to be evaluated by a reader — could be a professional script reader, a producer, an agent, or an executive. And that reader is going to take careful note of your characters and how you render them. As your reader considers your script, he or she will ask two essential questions: *Do I care about these characters and what happens to them?* and *Can this movie be cast with actors who will help sell it to an audience?* You're only going to make it past that reader if the answer to both of these questions is yes. That is to say, your lead and your supporting characters must be bulletproof.

That's the goal, bulletproof characters from your lead to your secondary and tertiary characters. We're going to use as our criteria for creating bulletproof characters these three considerations: Who is the best choice for a lead character given the concept I've come up with? Will a reader and audience be invested in my characters over the course of three acts and an hour and forty five minutes in the theater? And, finally, can these roles be cast with actors who will help sell the movie? Let's take them one by one.

The Tested Lead

As we posited in Chapter One, we believe your lead character should be one who stands to gain or lose the most given your concept. Our lead in the *The Whiz Kid,* a script about a 12 year-old who becomes a genius magically overnight, was a slacker kid, prone to shortcuts, to always taking the easy way out. In *Guam Goes to the Moon* it was a failed NASA astronaut whose reckless daring and irreverence cost him his shot at a space shuttle mission before the program was cancelled. In *The Family Man,* it was Jack Campbell, whose love for his college girlfriend Kate was eclipsed only by his professional ambition. Now he has the chance to reevaluate his priorities in light of the "glimpse" the movie provides into the life he would have had if he'd chosen differently back in his 20s. In *Old Dogs,* John Travolta and Robin Williams play Charlie and Dan, best friends and business partners who believe they've "beat the system," making it to their 50s without having to deal with any of the compromises and burdens parenthood entails. Then Dan learns he fathered twins during a brief post-divorce jaunt to Mexico with Charlie years ago and now the kids are coming to stay . . . indefinitely. Whether you're writing a big action tent pole, a concept-driven comedy, or a small indie drama, you want your lead to be the character or characters who will be most tested, most challenged and potentially rewarded by your premise. In the small, quiet, but enormously powerful drama *Manchester by the Sea,* a teenager whose father has died suddenly is left in the care of his uncle, the lead character played by Casey Affleck . . . who still blames himself for his role in the accidental death of his own children in a house fire years before. Small movie, high stakes. Your lead character, whether it's Liam Neeson's Bryan Mills in *Taken* or Saoirse Ronan in *Lady Bird,* should be tailor-made to suit your concept.

The Likable Lead

The second consideration you should have in mind is no less critical. Will people want to spend their time with these characters? If selling screenplays in Hollywood is an extended game of *Does it benefit me?* creating bulletproof characters is an extended response to the question, *Why should I care?* How can we care about what happens in your movie if we don't care about who it's happening to? And how can we care about the characters at the center of your story if we don't root for them, if we don't somehow like them? Now, you might bristle at that question. And for good reason. "Likable" is often mistaken, by writers and industry professionals alike, for flawless. And flawless characters are not interesting, nor do they have anything to learn from the stories we're trying to tell. There's also no evidence that flawed, even deeply flawed characters alienate viewers. In fact, the opposite is oftentimes true. Just look at movies with the word "Bad" in the title. *Bad Moms. Bad Teacher. Bad Santa.* Hit. Hit. Hit. Look at pretty much any role Jack Nicholson or Leonardo DiCaprio ever played. These are not choirboys. Look at Francis McDormand's Oscar-winning portrayal of Mildred in *Three Billboards Outside Ebbing, Missouri.* Badass.

So a likable lead is not the same thing as a flawless lead. But likability is important. It's two hours in the theater. Would you want to spend two hours in a theater, or anywhere for that matter, in the company of someone you don't like, or at least find interesting and entertaining? Readers won't finish screenplays with lead characters they find uninteresting or off-putting, and audiences likely won't show up for them at the theater either.

The Castable Lead

The key to building likable but flawed characters often lies in their core values and the way they express them. Rocky Balboa is a low-level collector for the local mob when he gets his opportunity to fight Apollo Creed in *Rocky*. A small-time boxer who makes his meager living collecting for the mob doesn't exactly scream "hero." But look at the way the character Sylvester Stallone created in that movie treats the vulnerable around him — Adrian and young Marie. Rocky is a protector who believes in and extends kindness, decency, even a dose of street wisdom. He's also a believer. Despite his circumstances, and his station and track record as a boxer, he believes that given the opportunity he can go the distance with the heavyweight champion of the world. He has a dream. We want him to win.

Your lead will be defined for us, to a point, within your first act, so we know what it means for them to be challenged by the change of circumstance you've introduced into their lives in the form of your concept and your first act break. But you are not finished with this character. Where do they go from there? There are many different kinds of journeys characters can take over the course of a screenplay. But if they haven't moved in some way by the end from where they were at the beginning, it calls into question the value of your entire story. Characters are revealed through action, through their response to challenges and temptation. They grow. They have arcs. One way to view these arcs and to use them to guide your story is to distinguish between what your character *wants* and what they *need*. You will define what they want at the end of act one. What they need may not be revealed until later in your story.

In *Black Panther*, Chadwick Boseman's T'Challa *wants* to take his rightful place as king of Wakanda. What he *needs*, though, is to earn his place as a true leader of his people, not just by defeating Killmonger, his antagonist, but by using the resources and capabilities of his small secluded country for the benefit of the larger world and suppressed and disadvantaged people everywhere. In *Ride Along*, Kevin Hart plays Ben, a security guard who *wants* his future brother in-law's blessing to marry his fiancé, Angela. But what he *needs* is to prove to himself to Angela's cop brother, played by Ice Cube, that he's strong and courageous enough to protect and care for her through all the trials and tribulations that married life presents. Luke Skywalker *wants* to get off Tatooine to begin a more exciting life away from his aunt and uncle's farm. What he *needs* is to overcome his impatience and assume his critical and unique place in something much bigger, a fight for peace and freedom . . . a fight, ultimately, between good and evil. Movie stars and character actors alike look for characters with strengths and weaknesses who make an impact at the same time that they have room to learn and grow.

So this is your lead — a flawed but likable character who will be most challenged by your premise, and one who has room to discover something about him or herself, with us, the reader and audience sharing in that discovery. Now what about the rest of your cast of characters?

The rest of your characters serve two essential purposes. The first, as we described earlier, is to populate and play a specific and necessary role in the world you've created. We know intuitively who many, if not most, of these characters are within minutes of coming up with our idea. If you're writing a heist movie, for example, you have your band of criminals, you have the people or the faces of the institution they're going to rob. You probably have a cop or FBI character. These characters fall naturally into two camps — the ones perpetrating the crime and the ones trying to stop or solve it. Remember, your movie is a debate — an argument among clashing interests and belief systems. Your criminals in your heist movie may be driven by pure greed, as they are in *Die Hard*. They may be driven by revenge, as they are in *Tower Heist*. Or by a sense of justice, as in the various movie versions of the Robin Hood story. Whatever the case, your cast of characters is spread between or among opposing forces. Your secondary and tertiary characters need to assume their position and represent one point of view or another within the debate staged by your screenplay. In *The Family Man*, Jack Campbell receives a phone message from his college girlfriend Kate on Christmas Eve. His assistant, Adele, sees a man who's put his career ahead of everything else in his life and who therefore will be spending Christmas alone. She urges him to return the call. Jack turns to his boss and mentor, Peter Lassiter, and asks his opinion. Lassiter replies, "Old flames are like old tax returns . . . put 'em in the file cabinet for three years, then you cut 'em loose."

When it comes to the role love should play in a person's life, in Jack's life, Adele is on one side of the argument and Lassiter is on the other. But Lassiter is Jack's mentor, and he confirms Jack's own instincts, and the decision Jack made earlier in life to pursue a professional opportunity abroad over beginning a life together with Kate. So Jack crumples the message from Kate and tosses it in the trash. Upshot? Jack wakes up the next morning in a glimpse of a life that might have been — lying in bed next to Kate in the house they share in Jersey with their two kids and a dog. Jack is on a journey of self-discovery, reexamining how he should prioritize his ambition in relation to the special love he shared with Kate. Every character that surrounds him, both in his New York life and in the life he finds himself living in New Jersey in his "glimpse," has a point of view on the subject. In the end, he has to determine his own answer, and then he has to fight as he — and we, the audience — never thought he would to get Kate to see the relationship the way he does now.

Surely, though, there must be more to building great characters than just a role in a story and a point of view. Don't I need to know all the intimate details of my character's life, from what they eat for breakfast to what brand of toothpaste they use? Shouldn't I write a 10-page character biography for each one in order to really capture their essence and bring them to life in my screenplay? No. Please, no!

The critical thing you must know about your characters is who they are and where they stand in relation to your idea and your lead. In time — and we'll get there in just a moment — some of these characters will emerge with stories of their own, B stories or subplots, that unfold alongside and in concert with your lead character. You'll fill out all of your characters with additional and relevant detail that will help bring them to life; details that suggest something meaningful and significant about their personalities and the role they play in the world you've created. What kind of car they drive, what they order in a bar . . . these can be revealing details, and revealing details are important and helpful in building memorable, impactful, multi-dimensional characters. A character who drinks Coors may be different from one who orders Macallan, or a Cosmopolitan . . . or a Shirley Temple. A character who drives a Ferrari is different from one who drives a Ford Fiesta. A character who wears custom suits and Italian shoes is different from one who dresses in Dockers and Merrills. But with apologies to Proctor & Gamble and Colgate-Palmolive, a character who brushes with Crest is not markedly different from one who brushes with Colgate. Some details matter. Others do not. Knowing the difference will determine whether you advance your effort to build a bulletproof screenplay filled with engaging characters or waste your time on fruitless exercises in an effort to instill false confidence.

Know your characters. If you're writing a scene in a bar you should have a pretty good idea what they drink. If they're pulling up to a house or to work, you should know what they're driving. You don't need to know if they had a crush on their 11th grade physics teacher unless that teacher is actually going to appear in your story. Don't waste your time on meaningless details of your characters' lives. Focus on what matters — your characters' roles in your story, and their perspectives. What you really need to know about most of them should fit nicely in a paragraph. If you'd like to write that up, by all means do. But if you're writing and writing and writing just for the sake of volume, to prove to yourself and your writing group or your instructor how much you know, how completely you've "mastered" your characters, you are tricking yourself into a false sense of security. But you will not trick anyone else. Ninety percent of what you're writing will never come into play in your script. The essence of your characters is exactly what your script reader will share about them. Add color. Do not waste your time on meaningless detail that will be imperceptible and insignificant to everyone but you.

Once you've arrived at a lead character that offers the best opportunity for your concept, and you've populated your story with a cast that also helps drive your narrative and dramatize the central thesis of your script, you can begin to imagine who's going to play these parts. Unless you're financing your movie yourself, or shooting it on your iPhone around the neighborhood, it can't just be your friends. To sell your script and get it made you need actors who have their choice of roles to sign on. Why should the actors you visualize in these roles (a good thing to do) even consider your script, let alone choose it from all the others being offered to them? Your actors are going to be reading your script with certain very specific questions in mind. What does their character get to do? What do they contribute to, or reveal about the story or the world? What makes them unique? Remember, actors are a critical link in the Hollywood chain you're relying on to sell and make your movie. *What's in it for them?*

To respond to this critical question, we offer a technique specifically designed to "amp up" each and every character and every story turn and escalation in your screenplay. As we know by now, checking off the first two boxes — creating characters with a clear and defined role and perspective — will provide a solid foundation for your screenplay. But you don't want just solid. Solid equals *Yeah I get it.* Solid is a writing sample. Maybe. You want bulletproof. And as far as actors are concerned, a bulletproof character is one who is active, who has interesting things to do in the movie, who endures challenges and responds in ways that are unexpected but authentic, revealing, and meaningful. These are some of the elements that go into a rich character. How do you ensure that your script affords these opportunities to your lead actor and all the other actors who will play a role in your movie? Our method for getting our characters to bulletproof is The Chart.

The Chart

Once we have our structure and characters, we feel like we have a pretty good handle on the script we're going to be writing. But we don't want to be caught writing scenes, or even planning scenes in an outline, that simply accomplish what we and our story are setting out to accomplish narratively. We want these scenes to live and breathe and feel dynamic, alive. So before we write a word of our script, before we even go to an outline or treatment, we make a chart*. On this chart we list all of our primary and secondary characters in our movie. Then we go down that list, one by one, *viewing the story we're telling through the eyes of each and every character.* We go through all three acts, every story turn and escalation, from the perspective of every character in our movie, writing down their experience of the story as it happens. This way, when we get to our outline and our script, we can view every scene as a confrontation between differing and sometimes opposing perspectives with characters that are vibrant, and action that is unexpected. This is the test that you want to pass at this stage of the writing process, and the chart will help get you there: Can you tell the story of your movie from the perspective of every character? If so, you are well on your way to producing a dynamic screenplay filled with roles actors will be eager and enthusiastic to play.

Let's return to our *Star Wars* one-pager and see what a chart might look in practice, using an iconic character from that iconic movie as our example. Let's see if our approach holds up by viewing the story of *Star Wars* from Han Solo's perspective:

The first thing we note is that Han does not appear in the first act of *Star Wars*. Act 1 belongs to Luke, he's our lead. The first act is further populated by critical characters Obi-Wan, R2-D2 and C-3PO. So Han won't make his appearance on our chart until we reach step number four. Number four on our chart typically corresponds with

---

* See figure 4.1.

what we call our page 45 turn or reversal. And guess what, if you look at the movie, we are in The Cantina on Mos Eisley, where Luke and Obi-Wan meet him, right at the forty-five minute marker. Chewbacca first appears talking with Obi-Wan at 45:30. And within the next few minutes, Harrison Ford appears and we get the line that introduced the world to a character who helped launch a franchise, "Han Solo. I'm Captain of the Millennium Falcon . . . .Chewie here tells me you're looking for passage to the Alderaan system."

Now, as Han makes very clear in the Cantina scene, he's into this mission for one reason and one reason only, the money. Turns out, as we discover the moment Luke and Obi-Wan leave him, Han has a debt to pay to Jabba the Hutt and there's a price on his head. He needs this gig. This should all be recorded on our chart where Han Solo's character lines up with step four.

In step five, their destination planet Alderaan's been destroyed and the giant mass in front of them that they thought was a moon turns out to be a deadly space station, the weapon used to destroy Alderaan, the Death Star. They're sucked inside where they discover Princess Leia is being held captive and that she's scheduled for execution. This means something very different for Han than it does for Luke.

For Luke, the mission has now gone from delivering a package — the R2 unit and the information within — to a rescue. That's a big escalation for his character and the story. But Han doesn't care about rescuing the Princess. That wasn't part of the deal. Meanwhile, all they're doing is attracting more attention from the Storm Troopers. There's an ongoing and deepening, character-based argument between Luke and Han about what they should do now and how they should do it. In the end, how does Luke convince Han to go along with his plan to rescue the Princess at further risk to their lives? He promises him money. "She's rich," says Luke. "How rich?" replies Han. Once again, Han's in it for the money, but the stakes — both financial and the stakes to life and limb — keep getting higher. That's Han Solo in step five, and that's just great storytelling.

Number six: The crew of the Millennium Falcon escapes the Death Star, but without Obi-Wan, who's sacrificed his life for the cause. This step places Luke and Han's differences in stark relief. For Luke, this is the low point — he's just lost his mentor. And if Leia's correct, their ship is being tracked and the Empire will soon know the location of the rebel base. But for Han, things are going better than he ever imagined — now he's going to get the money for delivering R2 to the Rebellion *and* for rescuing the Princess, one of the rebel leaders. He doesn't believe Leia knows what she's talking about; in fact, he's still pretty impressed with himself for having taken out the Storm Troopers who chased them in their escape from the Death Star. He is high when Luke is low. Leia, meanwhile recognizes his skill as a pilot and a fighter, and his charisma, but she couldn't be more turned off by his cynicism and his selfishness. It's all on the chart.

Just when we think the gulf in motivation and character between Han and the others could not be wider, we arrive at number seven. The rebel leaders have analyzed the plans to the Death Star and identified a vulnerability. The fighter pilots are manning their ships with their R2 units. Han has a chance to throw his lot in with the Rebellion. We know he has the skill and the talent. But he's got his money; that's what he came for. And he's prepared to ignore his better angels, not to mention the hopes of Luke and Leia, maybe even Chewbacca, by leaving just as the real fight is about to begin. It makes perfect sense. It's totally in keeping with his character from the moment we met him. And yet, it's disappointing. We want him to join this fight, and to be personally redeemed in the process.

Finally, at the story's climax in step number eight, Luke is closer than any other character at any other time in the movie to destroying the Death Star, and possibly the Empire along with it. But he has Vader on his tail, about to blow him to pieces when . . . Han pulls what's come to be called by some in the business "a Han Solo." He swoops in, seemingly from nowhere, surprising the audience and startling Vader, firing at his wingmen, clearing the way for Luke's shot, a bulls-eye. The Death

Star is destroyed and in our final step, number nine, Han and Chewie take their rightful places alongside Luke as a hero of the Rebellion.

What's happened here is that George Lucas has created a supporting ally character whose point of view contrasts with the hero-lead's so starkly that Han Solo actually emerges in many ways as a richer, more dynamic character than protagonist Luke. Luke is an innocent at the beginning where Han is a cynic. Han has farther to go as a character, a broader arc. And the casting of the movie reflects that. At the time George Lucas made *Star Wars* in 1977, Mark Hamill had done a lot of episodic television. He was not yet known for movie roles. Harrison Ford, on the other hand, had already made an impression in features, performing memorable roles in iconic movies, *American Graffiti*, directed by Lucas, and *The Conversation*, written and directed by Francis Ford Coppola. The results speak for themselves. Solo now has his own standalone movie, his own origin story being told as part of the *Star Wars* universe. This all began with an original screenplay and a story that could be told easily, clearly, and compellingly, with mounting dramatic stakes and tension, from the perspective of each and every character.

Now, there's still more to know and more to reveal about your characters. You're not done with them yet. You're going to need to find their voice and provide specific moments for each one of them to shine in your screenplay, helping to draw readers, actors, and ultimately an audience to them. We'll be returning to your characters and the on-going process of bringing them to life in the chapters ahead. But you should know enough, or decide enough, now to be able to take the next step in building out your story. So go ahead and make your own chart. Go character by character through your story and build your movie on a chart that, when complete, will reveal to you a picture of what a bulletproof screenplay can look like ...

Star Wars Chart (fig. 4.1)

	Luke	Han Solo	Leia	Obi-Wan	Darth Vader
1	Luke wants to leave Tatooine to become a fighter pilot for the Rebellion but his Uncle needs him on the farm.	Han's a cynical smuggler with a price on his head, desperate to repay his debt to Jabba the Hutt.	With the Republic and the Rebellion crumbling under pressure from the Empire, Princess Leia records a desperate plea for help from Jedi master Obi-Wan Kenobe.	The old Jedi master is living the life of a recluse on Tatooine as the battle between justice and evil wages on in the galaxy.	Determined to find the missing plans to the Death Star and crush the Rebellion, Vader seizes Princess Leia's ship and takes her prisoner.
2	Luke discovers the message from Leia in R2, pleading for help for the Rebellion from Obi-Wan.		Vader tries to get Leia to reveal the location of the Rebel base, but to no avail.	Obi-Wan rescues Luke from the Sand People, retrieves Leia's message from R2. He appeals to Luke to join him, but Luke has responsibilities at home.	Vador sends Storm Troopers to Tatooine to recover the plans.
3	When his aunt and uncle are killed by Storm Troopers, Luke joins Obi-Wan in the quest to deliver the Death Star plans to the Rebellion.		Even the injection of "truth serum" cannot compel Leia to reveal the location of the base.	When Luke's remaining family is killed, Obi-Wan becomes his mentor.	While Vader's Storm Troopers search for the missing plans, Vader himself tries to extract the location of the Rebel base from Leia.
4	Luke and Obi-Wan recruit smuggler Han Solo to deliver them and the plans inside R2 to Alderaan.	Luke and Obi-Wan offer Han the money he needs in exchange for safe passage to Alderaan.	The Empire destroys her home planet, Alderaan, and fierce Leia *still* will not reveal the location of the Rebel base.	Obi-Wan trains Luke in the ways of The Force and the use of the Lightsaber.	Vader's Storm Troopers are too weak-minded for Obi-Wan and the The Force. The Empire demonstrates the power of the Death Star by destroying the planet Alderaan.
5	With Alderaan destroyed and their ship held captive in the Death Star, Luke discovers Leia is being held there, as well, and is slated for execution. Now it's a rescue mission.	Han's not interested in the Rebellion or saving the princess, but Luke convinces him with the promise of more money.	"Rescued" by Luke and Han on the Death Star, Leia's unimpressed with their heroics until they can actually complete their mission—deliver those plans to the Rebellion.	Obi-Wan disables to tractor beam on the Death Star, aware that his presence means a confrontation with his former pupil, Vader.	Still determined to destroy the Rebel base, Vader is distracted when he senses the presence of his old master, Obi-Wan.

building bulletproof characters

	Luke	Han Solo	Leia	Obi-Wan	Darth Vader
6	Luke and co. rescue Leia but witness his mentor Obi-Wan cut down by Vader as they make their escape.	Han's feeling cocky —and maybe a little invested—as they escape the Death Star with the plans and the princess.	Leia feels the loss of Obi-Wan and she's concerned that their escape was too easy, that the Empire is tracking them.	Obi-Wan allows Vader to cut him down, facilitating his friends' escape and increasing his own power in the universe.	Vader cuts down Obi-Wan and has a homing beacon placed on Han's ship.
7	Luke delivers the plans to the Rebellion, but Obi-Wan is dead and Han, having received his reward, is abandoning the Rebellion to save his own skin.	Han eschews the opportunity to join the Rebel attack on the Death Star, leaving the Rebel base with Chewie and his reward money just as the fight's beginning.	Leia's right. The Empire has the location of the Rebel base, but analysis of the plans reveals a weakness in the Death Star.		With the Rebels scrambling to mount their unlikely attack, Vader and the Empire now have the location of the Rebel base and are minutes away from destroying it, and the Rebellion.
8	Han returns, providing Luke a clear shot at the Death Star. Luke lowers his screen and chooses to trust The Force to take his shot.	In a surprise turn, Han returns, saving Luke and clearing the path for his shot at the Death Star.	Leia monitors the Rebel attack. It's grim and worrisome...until the stunning return of Han Solo.	Obi-Wan's voice and influence remain with Luke as he urges him to trust The Force in his attack on the Death Star.	The threat from the Rebel pilots is real. Vader takes to his TIE fighter to personally take them out.
9	The Death Star is destroyed and Luke takes his place as a hero of the Rebellion.	Han takes his place alongside Luke as a hero of the Rebellion.	Leia proudly pins medals on Rebellion heroes Luke and Han (and Choowie), new allies in the fight for peace and justice in the galaxy.		Vader is seconds from destroying Luke and the last of the Rebel pilots when Han swoops in, sending Vader caroming off into space...

building the bulletproof outline

Remember back in Chapter Two when we said to enjoy finding your models, whiling away your time watching movies, because pretty soon the work was going to get harder? Well, if you were wondering when it was going to get harder, the answer is now. The reason it's going to get harder is that you're about to move from the theoretical movie you have in your head, and the broad schematics you have on paper in the form of your one-pager and chart, to a full-on comprehensive and practical rendering of your idea in the form of an outline, i.e., something you can actually write from. Now, you may say, *Why?! Why must I do an outline when I already know the structure of my movie and the major beats of my story from the perspective of every character?! Isn't that enough? Shouldn't that be enough?!* And we'll be honest.

In our two-plus decades in the business, we've met a few people who've tried writing without outlines. It can be done. These are people who are willing to write a whole draft and then throw it out and start all over again. Or forget what they've done altogether. That's what you have to be prepared to do if you write without an outline. Chances are, even a writer who works that way wouldn't recommend it to others. If you're really enthusiastic about your idea, and you care about it, you owe it the best and most complete preparation you can possibly do in the interest of the best result. You wouldn't want to live in a house that was built without a solid set of blueprints and you should not write your screenplay without a bulletproof outline. So let's roll up our sleeves and get to work . . .

There are two critical and essential differences between the information you already have about your movie and the information you will have once you complete the process of preparing and writing your outline. Your one pager and chart tell you *what* happens in your movie. Your outline will tell you *how* it happens. Also, your one-pager and chart are limited to the major escalations, turns and act breaks in your movie. Your outline will include the connective tissue, how you get from point A to point B. You do not want to be writing without the information you will have when you complete the tasks of this chapter. Return with us to the analogy of building a house and believe us when we tell you that there will still be plenty of room . . . plenty(!)for creative expression, instinct, and improvisation in the writing of your screenplay, even if, especially if, you write from a comprehensive outline or treatment. If you tell yourself that you know enough now to begin writing your script one of two things will happen (and perhaps both): You will hit a wall and become demoralized, realizing that you have no idea how to get where you want to go. Or you will go wildly off-track in your effort to follow your muse while also struggling to stick with the story you've already laid out. You'll be stuck at a fork in the road with no clear sense of which path to follow. We're not going to let that happen to you. We're going to take you through the writing of an outline that benefits from all the prep work you've done thus far and prepares you to write with confidence and enthusiasm.

The Meld

We're going to begin by taking your chart, in whatever form you've created it, and integrating the story and character information on it to tell your story chronologically. It will probably begin with your lead character, just as your one-pager does. If, however, there's a critical story beat, or information about one of your other key characters that precedes the introduction of your lead, by all means, put that down first. For example, *Star Wars* does not open with Luke Skywalker frustrated and impatient working for Uncle Owen and Aunt Beru on Tatooine, even though he's our lead and that's the first beat in his story, that's how we meet him. Rather, it begins with the Empire's Storm Troopers and Darth Vader boarding the rebel ship carrying Princess Leia and the plans to the Death Star. Because Leia and Vader, not to mention R2-D2 and C-3PO, are major characters in the movie, and Leia's placement of the plans to the Death Star inside R2-D2 and plea for help from Obi-Wan is a critical beat that provides the context for the entire story, that would go first, before we meet Luke. Look at your characters and where they are when we meet them and start listing these beats in sequence.

You'll notice early on, maybe even as soon as your first beat, that some story beats involve multiple characters with very different, perhaps even conflicting perspectives on the action — Vader and Leia, for example, in the sequence above. Congratulations! You're well on your way to a rich and dynamic screenplay. You want your scenes and sequences to involve characters with personal stakes tied to the outcome, and you want the stakes to be different and often conflicting for each of them. If your one-pager and your chart have helped you get to that place, that means they've worked.

You're going to come out of this exercise with some very long paragraphs listing the way a development in your story impacts multiple characters. Others will be brief and may involve only a single character. It's all good. It's all part of building out your story, seeing it from all points of view, and setting yourself up to write.

In 2005 we sold a pitch to ABC for a one hour drama called *9* — not to be confused with *The Nine*, which was also developed at ABC in 2005 and became a series that ran for twelve episodes the following year. Our *9* was about a diverse group of Angelenos, all of whom knew, through varied and personal revelatory experiences, the day of their death. Until they reached that day, each was essentially indestructible; they were practically superheroes. The concept was intended to create opportunities for all sorts of high-stakes action while it also invited us to explore life's big questions through the everyday lives of nine ordinary people with an extraordinary gift — they could not be killed before "their time." The idea also presented a real challenge in practice, i.e., how to introduce our studio and network partners, and ultimately our audience, to these nine very different characters, each living under very different circumstances, each with a secret that had unique implications and which they shared only with eight others in the world. How to approach this, to give each character their due, among the four storylines we'd conceived to sell the show to the network, and all in 42 pages?

Our producer partners on *9* were Bert Salke and Chris Brancato, film and television veterans who were no strangers to breaking stories with multiple leads and storylines. The approach that we all had in common, and that saved us enormous time and anguish in beating out our full pilot story, was the chart and the meld — nine characters across five acts and a teaser (that was the network standard format). Without the one-two punch of that technique, it's hard to know how we ever would have sold our pitch and wrapped our arms around all the potential story that could be mined from those nine characters in our pilot.

Movies are a little more forgiving than network television. You don't have commercial breaks to write to (hence three acts instead of five or six), and you have more than 42 minutes to tell your story. There's a little more time to breathe in feature films, space between some of the escalations and reversals. How you use that space will go a long way toward determining the strength of your script. Every moment on screen is precious (and expensive), even the quiet ones. And every moment should be essential in some way. These scenes and smaller moments that fill the space between the big twists and reversals are the ones we've not yet accounted for, and they are critical to building a bulletproof screenplay. By the time you're finished with your meld, you will have a reasonably full account of your story, told in sequence, from the perspective of every character who impacts, and is impacted by it. Now let's add some muscle!

Connective Tissue

Your chart and the meld you've fashioned from it have all of your major characters participating in a drama unfolding over the course of three acts. But they can't just magically appear in your most pivotal scenes without our knowing how or why they got there, or how they've been impacted by what they've been called upon to do. This is where the connective tissue of your screenplay comes into play. It's also where you'll find some of the greatest opportunities and biggest pitfalls. Let's return, once again, to our *Star Wars* example to illustrate what we mean.

Luke and Obi-Wan leave Tatooine on the Millennium Falcon with Han Solo and Chewbacca, C-3PO and R2-D2. The next significant beat in all of their stories is the realization that Alderaan, their desti-nation planet, has been destroyed. We know, intuitively, that we can't just leave Tatooine and cut immediately to their arrival at Alderaan, or what used to be Alderaan, in the very next scene. We need time on that ship. But we also don't want to watch our cast of characters just sitting around eating peanuts and sipping Pinot Grigio. Something must happen on that ship, but what? How does George Lucas get us from point A to point B? The answer is on the chart. It lies in the disparate characters who find themselves suddenly and unexpectedly stuck together — Obi-Wan, the mentor, Luke his eager apprentice, and Han Solo, the mercenary. So what happens? Obi-Wan attempts to train Luke in the use of his light saber and the ways of The Force. Han weighs in with his cynical attitude about the Jedi that will inform and explain his response to every challenge and opportunity ahead. It's a great scene on the Falcon that helps draw us further inside the world Lucas has created. By the time they discover Alderaan's been destroyed and they're fighting to escape the Death Star, we know each of them a little bit better and we like them all, including Han, a little bit more. Our investment in these characters, their predicament, and their mission is increasing with every scene.

So connective tissue is not idle conversation among characters. It's not comic or action set pieces just for the sake of set pieces (though set pieces are important, in fact they're next up on our agenda). Connective tissue helps to advance your story and your characters, just as the major turns and escalations do. Take a look at the story and characters before you in your meld and ask yourself what has to happen from one turn to the next in order for your audience to be oriented in this story, in order to get out what's necessary in the journey of your characters, and in order to take maximum advantage of your concept. It's time to beat out exactly what's going to happen in your movie. If you've done your homework thus far, these should not be random decisions. Your characters and story turns, and the dramatic case you're building in your screenplay, should go a long way toward determining the action, the connective tissue in between the steps reflected in your one-pager and your chart.

Subplots: B Stories, C Stories, and "Runners"

As you explore the worlds and lives of your characters, new details will emerge in your story. Whether you're writing an ensemble movie or a movie with a single lead, each character you create will come to the situation you've put them in with his or her own unique set of circumstances. They have lives and stories of their own, seemingly disconnected from the concept that's driving your movie idea. Some of these stories will continue to develop alongside your A Story. Han Solo's debt to Jabba the Hutt is the perfect example. He comes to Luke and Obi-Wan's request for transport with this desperate need for money already in place. It informs every decision he makes from this point forward in the story, through his final act of friendship and heroism at the end of the movie. The key to formulating successful subplots is in recognizing that they are not, or should not be, in fact, disconnected from the rest of your movie at all. They're actually an organic part of your larger idea. Subplots are not separate stories, arrived at arbitrarily for color, that just happen to collide with what's happening to your lead characters.

B and C stories are opportunities to challenge and to bolster the central thesis of your movie and the goals of your leads. If your subplots are not linked thematically and narratively to your A story, you've not conceived them correctly or thought them through sufficiently. Find interesting lives and voices for your supporting characters, but make sure their stories converge with the central drama and that they contribute in some fashion to the debate that's playing out in your script. If you get to your third act and find yourself suddenly with all sorts of seemingly unrelated loose ends to tie up, it's likely because you set B and C stories in motion that weren't properly integrated from the beginning. The idea and theme of your movie have as much to say about the smaller stories that play out within it as your subplots and ancillary characters have to say about your A story.

The more you drill down in the lives and personalities of your supporting characters, the more opportunities you'll find for motifs, callbacks, and comic runners. Even if you're not writing a comedy, it can be tremendously helpful and appealing to have a character or characters with a comic perspective and voice to lighten the mood, break the tension, and provide a little comic relief. These comic "runners" often play out in your smallest stories, maybe just three or four scenes spread throughout the movie, but they can make all the difference. Look, for example, at the way Lil Rel Howery's character Rod, the TSA agent, contributed to the success of *Get Out*. Rod, lead character Chris's best friend, rants and raves about his conspiracy theories throughout the movie to anyone who'll listen — Chris, Chris's girlfriend Rose, the police. Of course everyone, including the audience, thinks he's nuts. Until, it turns out, he isn't. Where would *Get Out*, or lead character Chris, be without the boundary pushing perspective and comic voice of Rod? As you look at your chart, and begin to consider your outline, see if you can identify characters and opportunities to punctuate the action and enhance the experience of the movie you're writing. Conceive of all the stories in your script so that they converge in an unexpected way and are fully integrated in your third act, and you will deliver a satisfying and powerful conclusion to a bulletproof screenplay.

The Outline

This is where the rubber hits the road, friends. If the meld you created from your chart and your one-pager was a largely mechanical process, and coming up with your connective tissue was like a more creative version of connect the dots, writing your outline is really going to put you and your determination to see this through to the test. Outlines usually aren't fun. They don't come with the rewards that actual scene writing often has to offer. They're sometimes easier to get through if you're working with a partner and trading ideas and running dialogue is a part of the process. This is one reason people choose to work with partners. Of course the downside is that two people procrastinating before outline or script writing can take twice as long as one — or longer! We once spent eight solid months watching construction trucks dig out a giant hole for an underground parking structure across from our office. For the most part, though, whether you're doing it yourself or with a partner, translating what's going to happen in your script to how it's going to happen is an opportunity to test both creativity and commitment. And you are ready.

We can offer some general guidance for approaching your outline, but for the most part you're going to have to go into it armed with the ideas and information you've already accumulated about your script and your own creative instincts. Which is fine. By now you actually know an enormous amount about your movie. You know your cast of characters and their respective points of view. You know your story and how it's going to play out over three acts, both in its broadest strokes and the connective tissue in between. What you need now, more than anything else, is your imagination and inspiration. For some this may be the hardest part. For others, this is the moment you've been waiting for, the step in the process when you can finally stop listening to the voices (including ours) telling you what you can and can't do and start unleashing the artist within. In either case, it's time to have at it.

Some things to remember as you expand your list of story beats into ideas for, and approaches to, active scenes: remember that actions speak louder than words. As in life, what your characters do, how they respond to their circumstances through action, will tell us more about them than what they say. A character who describes himself as a very honest person probably just arouses our suspicion, whereas a character who finds $10,000 on the street and devotes himself to returning the money to whoever lost it earns our respect and our investment in their efforts. The critical difference is that we, the audience, are the ones deciding that the character is honest. That's the slight of hand you're looking to perform here, beginning with your outline and through the writing of your screenplay. You've made the decisions about these characters and their role in the story. But you want to render them in such a way that we, the readers of your script and the audience for your movie, are the ones assessing and judging the characters, deciding who should win and who should lose. The more you give us that opportunity, the more invested we become in the story. This is part of the magic of screenwriting and when it works it's incredibly powerful. This outline is the plan for your grand illusion.

Another tip: Keep your story simple. Your characters should be rich, and the stakes of your story high, the action unpredictable. But over-complicating the plot of your movie will only diminish it. Don't add layers of unnecessary plot and action just to keep us guessing and on our toes. If you've got reversals and turns every fifteen pages or so in your second act, throwing in more plot is likely not necessary or helpful. In fact, just the opposite may be true. Your outline should be proof of concept, and proof of theme. Put yourself, once again, in the position of attorney, arguing the case for what you're trying to prove in your story. Does every scene you're envisioning help further your case? Is each one necessary to connect the pieces of your argument? If not, you probably need to lose it, no matter how colorful a scene it may be in your mind. It's a distraction at best, and it will likely just be cut later. Or it will survive and readers will be left to assess your script based on these scenes you've written that don't really contribute to it. Put another way, we want your outline to be bulletproof!

Avoid the impulse to have information communicated through phone conversations or meetings over coffee. You can meet your friends for coffee and you can get information about family members from your mother on the phone. These are movies. We go to them because things happen in more interesting ways than they typically happen to us. Ask yourself as you're approaching each necessary scene and sequence, *What is the most interesting way that this can happen?* Take the question seriously. If you don't have the answer go for a walk around the block, go get a cup of coffee . . . pray on it. Do whatever helps clear your head and spark your imagination. Of course, sometimes the answer is . . . they meet for coffee, or breakfast, or a beer, because this is what people actually do in real life in this situation, this is what's most authentic. Jerry Maguire was fired in a restaurant over lunch. That scene worked — and it was very deliberately conceived. Again, don't be too religious about these rules and guidelines, just be thoughtful, intentional, creative. When you find an approach that excites you and feels most authentic to you, chances are your reader and your audience will respond the same way.

You can use any tool or approach to outlining that you like, as long as you avoid shortcuts and come out with a document that will actually serve you when it's time to write. Our outlines would be pretty much illegible to anyone but us. They're written in cramped handwriting, from back to front in notebooks or sections of notebooks often used for other purposes. They include story and character notes, and lines of possible dialogue, but they're not remotely suitable for public consumption. They're good for one thing and one thing only, guiding us day in and day out as we move from one scene to the next in our screenplay. That said, for the purposes of illustration, let's take a look at what a piece of an outline looks like for us.

Here's the first act of *The Family Man*, as imagined before the script was written and before any director or actor had come aboard:

```
- We open on JACK and KATE at Kennedy Airport 13 years
ago. A tearful goodbye. She's made a mix-tape for him
— "Every one of these songs will remind you of me in a
slightly different way." It's hard for Jack to leave
. . . but it's time. Then, just as he turns to enter
the jetway, "Wait." Kate tells him she has a bad feel-
ing—suddenly their decision that he would take this
position in London seems wrong. They had a plan, but if
they really want to do something great they should flush
```

the plan and start their lives together today. "I don't know what that life looks like but I know it has the both of us in it. And I choose us." Jack assures her. "I love you Kate. And one year in London's not gonna change that. A hundred years couldn't change that." And off he goes . . .

- Dissolve To: Present Day. Jack wakes up in his spectacular Manhattan apartment next to a beautiful woman . . . who is not Kate. He wants to see her again—tonight. But it's Christmas Eve, she'll be with family. Jack's not oblivious to Christmas, it's just not a priority like it is to most.

- Jack's a Master of the Universe, he relishes every moment of his morning ritual, getting dressed in a closet the size of a small house, filled with handmade suits and Italian shoes . . .

- He rides down in the elevator with his neighbor, MRS. PETERSON — they have a nice rapport, he tosses off some casual financial advice to TONY the doorman . . . they like him.

- Jack races through Manhattan in his Ferrari, pulls up outside P.K. Lassiter & Assoc., where a valet takes his car . . .

- In the boardroom at Lassiter & Assoc. Jack's walking the team through the biggest deal in company history, a $30 billion pharmaceutical acquisition. V.P. ALAN MINTZ is eager to get home to his wife and kids for

Christmas. For Jack, the real holiday is the day this deal goes through . . .

- The meeting lets out late. Jack's assistant ADELE hands him his phone messages. There's one from Kate. Adele can tell there's something there but when she asks Jack about it his perspective on what happened 13 years ago at the airport is skewed — in hindsight he views her appeal to him to stay as an attempt to keep him from realizing his potential, from being all he could be. Adele wants to get Kate on the phone but Jack stops her. Then Peter Lassiter himself enters — lots of gravitas but it's clear Jack is favored, the heir apparent. The buyer in Jack's deal is getting nervous, it's a lot of money. Jack tells Adele to cancel Christmas plans with his aunt and book him a flight to meet with the buyer. Then he asks his mentor's opinion on the subject of Kate — "Old flames are like old tax returns. You keep 'em in the file cabinet for three years and then you cut 'em loose . . . " Jack tosses the message.

- . . . still, something about this night — maybe it's Christmas Eve, maybe it's that call from Kate — Jack doesn't feel like going home, not yet, not alone . . . He stops off for a drink near the office, strikes up a conversation with SULLY, the colorful character sitting next to him at the bar.* They get to talking

---

* This character and scene was later replaced when the director came aboard and saw an opportunity for a more contemporary feeling entry to the special world of the movie.

about regrets and Jack insists he has no regrets, how could he, his life is exactly as he wants it to be . . .

- Jack goes to sleep in his Manhattan apartment, but when he wakes up . . .

- He's in the "master" bedroom of a decidedly middle class three bedroom, two and half bath house in Jersey. There's a woman next to him . . . is it the woman from last night? It is not. This woman is much closer to his own age. It's Kate. WTF?! Then a little girl barrels in — six years old, carrying her 18-month-old baby brother. ANNIE. She starts jumping on the bed, singing, she wants to open the Christmas presents . . .

- Jack freaks out, he can't get out of there fast enough. He races out of the room, and out of the house, running straight into . . .

- BIG ED and LORRAINE, Kate's folks. Big Ed talks like he's from Texas even though he's from Paramus. Lorraine drinks too much, she was over it years ago but she loves the grandkids. These two are a little much on a good day, all the more so for Jack today when he hasn't seen them in 13 years and he feels like he's in the middle of a bad, extended acid trip.

- Jack grabs the keys to the family mini-van (insult to injury), races into the city to his building. But Tony the doorman doesn't recognize him and won't let him in. He sees Jack in his sweatpants on a rant and mistakes him for a homeless person. Mrs. Peterson, returning from walking her dog, doesn't recognize

Jack either. Jack's desperate . . . "We fought side by side for garbage disposals!" Now Jack's really being pushed to the edge. Tony threatens to call the cops, Jack responds, threatening to report them both to the coop board . . .

- Jack heads to the office, but the security guard there doesn't recognize him and won't let him in, either. He tries to insist he's president of P.K. Lassiter & Assoc., but when he points to the building directory it's not his name listed as company president below CEO Lassiter's, it's teddy bear Alan Mintz's!

- Jack emerges from the office lost and confused, with no clue what's going on or how to proceed, except for the key to the family mini-van double parked outside. He returns to the car, and to Jersey, now stuck in a life that seems worse in every way to him than the one he built for himself since leaving Kate at that airport 13 years before . . .

                                    END ACT ONE

A few observations before we wrap up our discussion of outlines. Notice that the central argument of the movie begins in the very first scene, when Kate appeals to Jack to abandon their more reasonable plan in favor of an uncertain life path that they know for sure will at least have both of them in it. Jack leaves despite Kate's appeal, but whether or not he's actually the better for it continues to be a matter of some dispute thirteen years and just a few scenes later as his assistant Adele encourages him to return Kate's call. Peter Lassiter might as well be the voice that called Jack away from Kate to London in the first place, and Jack heeds that voice, once again, all these years later, even with the benefit of hindsight. He has to be forced, through this "glimpse," to seriously entertain the possibility that there might have been a cost to his decision to put the relationship on hold while he pursued the business opportunity that's obviously worked out so well for him. This debate continues through the entire movie, right up to the very last scene, where the tables are finally turned and it's now Jack who has to provide a glimpse of sorts to Kate. She's leaving for Paris, and he argues for her to stay, even if it's just long enough for a cup of coffee with him. Pretty much every character in the movie, those we meet in act one and those we meet only later in act two, have a point of view somewhere along the spectrum of opinion in this debate over what should prevail when love and professional ambition conflict.

Look also at the bones of the first act, the beats that you'd find on the one pager and the chart, and the scenes that serve as connective tissue. We open with the choice that sets the entire story in motion. The expressions of love between Jack and Kate — he does love her, he makes no secret of that — invest us in the two of them being together from the very beginning. After a series of scenes that provide a portrait of Jack's life present day, without Kate — connective tissue — we get the phone message. That's page 10 in our screenplay. Jack then debates with Adele and Lassiter and has his encounter with Sully, our guardian angel character. By page 19 Jack wakes up next to Kate in the house in Jersey. Jack then makes his escape in the minivan. He stops at his apartment and his office. More connective tissue, all logical and necessary for the character, and grist for the comedy mill. By page 28 he's back in the house in Jersey, with Kate and the two kids, in a life he never chose but which he apparently cannot escape. End of act one. Each scene in the first act outline serves a specific purpose and helps advance story, character, and theme.

The road to getting *The Family Man* made felt long to us, and the path was not without significant obstacles. It took almost five years. We lost our first director, Curtis Hanson, with whom we worked closely on the script for several months, when he decided to direct

Wonder Boys, a movie that was more personal to him, instead. Months would go by when there seemed to be no activity at all, no effort to get the movie back up and running. In the end, though, the story and the screenplay survived the vicissitudes of Hollywood because all the major stakeholders — the producers, the directors, the studio, and ultimately the actors — found something in it that was important to them, that was worth taking on, putting effort into, and ultimately fighting for. The movie had a chance, and succeeded, in large part because it was conceived with enthusiasm and written with love and a genuine desire to make something that would be wonderful, magical, romantic, inspiring, and fun. The finished film had its fans and its detractors. As the years pass, there seem to be more and more of the former and fewer of the latter, which is very nice. No matter how deliberate and diligent you are in your process, some scripts just prove to be more bulletproof than others. This one always seemed to have a little extra dose of pixie dust on it.

Outline, Treatment, or Pitch Document

The form the document you'll ultimately write from takes may depend on how you're stationed in the business and what you can reasonably hope to accomplish with the document. If you're already an accomplished writer, with an agent and some script sales under your belt, or maybe even a produced credit, you may be in a position to pitch your movie. Pitches used to be more common and sold more regularly than they do now for the simple reason that studios used to produce and distribute more original movies, so they bought and developed many, many more original ideas. Now that studios are relying more on intellectual property in an effort to maximize profits and limit financial risk, it's hard to sell a pitch without significant elements attached — a big director or in-demand actor, or both. If you happen to be in a position to pitch to such people, you may want to write your outline up in the form of a pitch document, something you can deliver either by reading, memorizing, or presenting in a more extemporaneous way using your outline for cues. We pitched *The Family Man* from a document we memorized that ran over nine pages. The pitch was about a half hour long, which was a ridiculous thing to do, even in 1995. But we'd written out whole speeches from the movie, including Jack's closing "We have a house in Jersey . . . !" speech to Kate at the airport when he tries to provide her with a little glimpse into the life he's seen of the two of them together. If you're in a position to pitch your movie, and it's your plan to do that, you need to make sure that you're giving your buyer as complete a sense of your movie as you can. The goal of the pitch is for the buyer to feel as if they've just seen the movie from beginning to end, preferably in twenty minutes or less. Unless you're James Cameron, anything longer may try their patience.

You may wonder if it's possible to write your outline up in narrative form as a movie treatment and sell that, so you can put less work in upfront and be paid to write the script. The answer is no. That will not happen. Producers and financiers who work in the mainstream movie business do not buy movie treatments, and they don't often use them to attract interest from other parties. For the most part, only your finished screenplay will serve you as something you can actually sell. However, if you're working with a manager or a producer to develop your idea into a script,* it may be very helpful to write your outline up in narrative pages so that you can get the most meaningful feedback from them. The same is true if you're working on your idea in the context of a class or writers group — by all means, in that case go ahead and write up a treatment. Whatever helps. Lay out your story in seven to ten pages. Fifteen. Does it hold the interest of people who are not related or married to you? This is another opportunity to test

---

* Note that the Writers Guild of America has very specific rules about the relationship between writers and producers and what can and cannot be done without a contract and payment. This applies, of course, to writers who are already members of the WGA.

the viability of your idea and your approach to it. If those who are invested in your success and your idea are at all tentative, now's the time to right the ship, or abandon it altogether if that doesn't seem possible. Remember, you're not writing this story for yourself, you're writing if for some complete stranger sitting in a multiplex in Beijing. Do not proceed until your pitch document, treatment, or outline has all it takes to entice a producer, a director, a cast of in-demand actors, and a studio executive or financier and their marketing department! Don't think about submitting your treatment to agents and producers in the hopes of breaking in. It's not done and you are not the exception to the rule. Do what the rest of us did and write your screenplay and make it great. Make it bulletproof.

the bulletproof
set piece

In the summer of 2005, our agent set up a meeting for us with *Wedding Crashers* producer Andrew Panay. *Crashers* had just been released in July and was already well on its way to earning over $200 million at the domestic box office, and Panay was riding pretty high. We, on the other hand, were experiencing a lull in our career with projects that just didn't seem to be gaining any traction. We knew a lot of producers in town by this point, especially comedy producers, but we'd never met Panay. He did not disappoint. Clad in the skinniest of jeans and tightest of tees, with bulging muscles and a wild mane of hair that called to mind the biblical Samson, Panay spoke a language we'd never quite heard before, a mash-up of hipster lingo, comedy-speak, and a smattering of expressions all his own. He was also highly energetic, very passionate and creative, a real force of nature. We talked generally for a few minutes, trading stories of how we came up in the business, and then we got to talking ideas. Maybe we had some at that point, maybe not. This was just a general "get to know you" meeting, not a formal pitch meeting. But Panay had an idea, or at least the seed of an idea, to share. According to California law, he told us, fathers of children twelve months or younger are entitled to six weeks of paid paternity leave. He wanted to do a comedy about a guy who's exhausted all his vacation and personal days at work and manufactures a fake paternity leave using someone else's newborn in order to go on vacation with a friend. We liked this idea. This felt very much up our alley — an older (though not necessarily more mature) version of our character from *The Whiz Kid* taking a shortcut and learning something unexpected about himself and about life when he's forced to face the consequences. We told Panay we'd see him in a few weeks.

We returned to his office a few weeks later, as promised, armed with a six-page pitch document. It was the product of everything we've spelled out thus far — a strong concept we'd not seen before, a winning lead who stood to gain and lose the most based on that concept, great iconic comedy models, a structure that worked beautifully on a one pager, a chart that pit our lead against characters with opposing points of view and interests, and a narrative pitch document that put it all together from beginning to end in just the right tone. Bulletproof.

We felt good, confident. We'd sold *Guam Goes to the Moon* on a pitch, *The Family Man* on a pitch. We'd pitched approaches to writing assignments that had resulted in years of lucrative jobs. We knew what we were doing. Our take on *Paternity Leave* was a winner.

Panay was excited to receive us. He had a lot of enthusiasm for this idea and was eager to hear what we had to say. So we pitched away. All three acts. It probably took a good twenty, twenty-five minutes. When we were finished, we felt like we'd handed Panay a gift — he gave us a concept and we returned a few short weeks later with a completely worked out, fully realized movie, ready to write. This was his response: "Guys. First act, perfect. Third act, genius . . . problem is, I didn't hear a word you said in between. What's the second act? Where are the set pieces?!"

"I didn't hear a word you said." It wasn't clear to us at the time if he meant this literally or figuratively. Probably literally, but it doesn't matter. We'd spent a good ten to fifteen minutes pitching a second act that simply did not penetrate. He hadn't heard a word. Our pitch didn't work for him because we didn't have these things called set pieces . . . .

What's a Set Piece?

Set pieces. Comedies have them, action movies have them, thrillers have them, sci-fi movies have them, adventure movies have them, horror movies have them . . . even dramas have them, they're just a little quieter, but no less impactful. Like pornography, set-pieces may be difficult to define with real precision, but you know them when you see them . . . E.T. and Elliot making their escape at the end of *E.T.*, flying with the boys on their bikes before the image of the giant moon, Tom Hanks playing that oversized piano with Robert Loggia on the floor of FAO Schwarz in *Big*, Harrison Ford shooting the master swordsman in *Raiders of the Lost Ark* . . . These are the scenes you can refer to simply as "The _____ Scene" and everyone knows what you're talking about. The "French Toast Scene" in *Ordinary People*, or the scene where De Niro as Jake La Motta tells Joe Pesci to punch him as hard as he can in *Raging Bull*. And while we're talking De Niro . . . "You talkin' to me?" That's right, under the right circumstances, a set-piece can be nothing more than a guy talking to himself in the mirror. A successful set piece provides, in a single energizing scene or sequence, proof in action of the big screen potential of your movie. Trailer moments.

The right set piece will generate enthusiasm and buzz for your script and elevate the experience of reading your screenplay and seeing your movie. It will also deliver to the marketing people, who have a vote in what does and does not get bought and made at any studio, a reason to give your project a thumbs up. When production and marketing executives read and see set pieces they know they can cut trailers and sell your movie. Conceiving and writing good set pieces is a critical part of writing a bulletproof screenplay.

Our scripts and movies, even then, had set pieces, too. We couldn't have reached the point of our first meeting with Panay ten years into our career without them. But what we hadn't accounted for — and the chart-topping success of *Wedding Crashers* was as responsible for this phenomenon as it was emblematic of it — was that there was a real and palpable transition taking place in movies generally, and comedy in particular, at this time. With competition for eyeballs on big and small screens becoming ever more intense, studios were swinging for the fences now, pretty much every time out. And swinging for the fences meant big, bold, envelope-pushing set pieces that would get people talking. And Tweeting. Of course the best and most sophisticated comedies of the 1980s and 90s had set pieces. The difference was that those movies were accented by set pieces, not driven by them. Things were changing. Compare *Working Girl* with *Bridesmaids*, *Tootsie* with *We're the Millers* or *Horrible Bosses*. By asking *"Where are the set pieces?!"* Panay was, in his own inimitable way, inviting us into the present.

We returned to our office from the pitch a little confused, and deflated. It didn't make sense to us that our second act didn't register when it had been so carefully conceived and so effectively set up and paid off in the first and third acts. But this was the producer of *Wedding Crashers*, at that time the number one R-rated comedy of all time. Surely he knew what he was talking about. So we took another look at our second act. All the story was there, the character arcs were playing out just as we thought they should, there were fun scenes of our lead struggling to navigate his desire for time off with the actual hands-on care of this child that our page 45 reversal demanded of him. And he was falling for the mother, a college friend and real over-achieving

84

"type A" personality he'd never thought of "in that way" before. But Panay was right. We were missing big set-pieces. We had witty dialogue and fun scenes, but they weren't the kinds of scenes you'd run out of the theater —or worse, sit in the theater during the movie — and text your friends about.

So we got to work. We talked through the second act and looked for any place that we could ratchet up the action, create situations that would take the story we already had to a more extreme place, still rooted in story and character, just . . . more. And we found places. Several of them, in fact. We brainstormed for the most fun and funny set-pieces we could come up with at every turn in the story until we found ourselves literally falling on the floor laughing with tears in our eyes. * And that's the moment it all clicked. That's the moment we really understood, not just intellectually but in our guts, what set pieces are and how invaluably the right set piece can contribute to a pitch or a script.

Building Your Set Pieces

Return to your list of models. Go online. Look at the trailers for those movies. Do you see snippets of set pieces that you recognize, signature moments that have made their way into the collective consciousness of the movie-going public? Think about the trailer to the movie you're writing now. What should be in there that you haven't already accounted for? Do the job of the marketing person, see your screenplay through their eyes, and you will go a long way toward thrilling your reader and your audience. Come up with some good set pieces, try one for the first and third act each and then several for the second act. Watch *Raiders of the Lost Ark* again. That movie opens and closes with set pieces and has numerous memorable set pieces in between, all of

---

* See pages 158-161, The Breast Pump Sequence from *Paternity Leave*, draft date 5-7-10. Property of New Line Cinema. Used by permission.

them bolstering the characters and enhancing the story and the experience of watching it all play out. That's what the good set pieces do — they thrill by *contributing* to story and character (like the oversized piano set-piece in *Big*), they do not distract or divert from character or narrative. Set pieces shouldn't be tangents or lateral moves in your story, they should be part of the necessary connective tissue jacked up to strengthen the dramatic argument you're putting forward.

You may find the most effective set pieces often play out in front of large groups of people — think of Matthew Broderick in "The 'Twist and Shout' Scene" in *Ferris Bueller's Day Off*.* That's an approach to consider if it's organic to your story, but beware: Placing a scene or an action in front of a large group does not automatically make it a set piece. Don't fall into the trap of imitating monster scenes you've seen play out successfully in other movies and expect them to deliver for you in the same way. One of the things that makes set pieces work is their originality, the fact that we've not seen them before. "The Pie Scene" in *American Pie*. In other words, while you may be able to discern key ingredients to building an effective set piece, there is, once again, no formula.

Return to your outline. Look at the scenes in which you introduce your main characters. Is there a way to take those scenes to the next level, to raise the stakes in them, to make them more active, more funny/scary/exciting/dramatically tense and impactful? Go through each phase of your story this way, look at your big turns and your connective tissue. How can you make the action more compelling? How can you define your characters even more clearly by representing their choices more in high-stakes action than dialogue? If there are opportunities to elevate scenes to set pieces without violating the tone of your script, take them, whether they're in your first act, second or third, keeping in

---

* Writer-director John Hughes was a set piece genius, by the way. Take a look at any of his comedies for a master class in the importance and effectiveness of set pieces and how to approach them.

mind, of course, that even roller coasters have a slow and steady climb before a big, thrilling drop. You want set pieces in your movie, but set pieces work best as the payoff following a period of anticipation. *Meet the Parents* had many great and memorable set pieces, but they worked in large part due to the genuine pathos writers Greg Glienna & Mary Ruth Clarke, Jim Herzfeld and John Hamburg built into the screenplay, and which Ben Stiller, Robert De Niro and Jay Roach brought to life in making the movie. Build out your set pieces, remembering as you do so that the impact of any action is determined largely by what it reveals about your characters. Set pieces that are not grounded in reality will rarely, if ever, be referred to as "The _____ Scene." Your set pieces will not work if we don't understand and care about your characters and their goals and aspirations.

On September 28, 2005 we went on what our *Paternity Leave* producer Andrew Panay called "the tour," taking our now set piece-infused pitch to every studio in town. We began at New Line Cinema. From there, we continued to Walt Disney Pictures and pitched executives there. We got through one more pitch at Paramount, one last stop on the tour, before our agents called and told us to stay put. Both New Line and Disney were going to make offers and we were not to continue to Universal, our next stop. We waited on the Paramount lot with Panay through the lunch hour while our agents went back and forth between competing offers from Disney and New Line. The day was, and remains, one of the most exciting of our career, an unforgettable experience that culminated in the largest pitch or spec sale we'd ever made.

Would our earlier version of the *Paternity Leave* pitch without the set pieces have sold? Maybe. Possibly. It certainly recalled earlier scripts we'd written that executives around town had fondness for — *The Whiz Kid, Guam Goes to the Moon, The Family Man* . . . heartfelt and funny scripts, each one of them. But hearing the pitch with big, bold, organically built in set pieces made executives feel like they'd actually seen the movie, experienced the fun of it, and knew how to sell it.

They were meetings that inspired studio presidents to pick up the phone and say to their business affairs executives and our agents, "*I've gotta have it.*"

Respect your characters. Respect your story. Respect your tone. And find a way to introduce compelling, effective set pieces into the outline for your script. That's it, friends, the last bit of guidance we have to offer in your prep work. Pick your spots and conceive some choice set pieces to inject into that outline, and then, when you're finished, let's sit down to write a bulletproof screenplay.

writing the bulletproof screenplay

When someone we know, or someone who knows someone we know, asks us to read their script, we usually agree, with one important caveat. Unless you're a close friend or family member we offer to read exactly as any other industry professional would, i.e., we open to page one with the hope that we'll read all the way to the end, excited to pass along a phenomenal screenplay and help to introduce the world to an as-yet undiscovered talent. If, however, the script loses us at any point before the end — and that point may be page 5 or page 75 — we'll stop reading, just as any other industry professional would. We'll share with the writer where we stopped and why, along with any other observations and insights we can from what we've read, but we will not continue with a script we've already given up on. We approach reading this way for several reasons. The first is purely practical. We have to protect our time. We have our own writing to do, and sometimes scripts to read for work. We also have families and other commitments outside of work, so our time is limited. *Just like every other industry professional who agrees to read your work.* Second, the writer should understand where the bar is when he or she asks someone who is not a close personal friend or family member to read their script. You're asking for potentially hours of your reader's time. It shouldn't be taken lightly. Finally, you don't generally get multiple shots with the same reader unless that reader genuinely believes there's potential for your script and thinks they can help you realize that potential, so you have to be really, really discerning about who you ask and when in the process you ask them to read. You want to ask the right person with the right script at the right time. And you don't want to blow it. Of course, many people read various drafts of numerous scripts that we wrote before we eventually sold our first spec. We made sure we positioned ourselves in the business in such a way that we would have access to more than one reader, which you should too. We'll be talking more about that in the next and final chapter when we discuss how to sell your script. But none of this diminishes the importance of valuing every reader and every read. There's a lot of wonderful freedom that comes with writing, but the basic framework and objective of the endeavor is no different from what we've been emphasizing every step of the way. Don't Lose The Reader. This is the focus of this chapter, to offer an approach to writing your screenplay with that one simple, yet critical, goal in mind. Which is really just another way of saying, be bulletproof.

If you're struggling with the idea that you're writing for a reader, rather than for your own creative edification, chances are you put this book down a long time ago. If you're still with us, it means you understand that the folks who can actually buy your script will not read it unless someone they trust tells them they must. If you want to bypass the system and position yourself to get an automatic read from a studio president, the best way to do it is to win an Oscar, or maybe a Pulitzer Prize, or write a movie that earns $600 million at the box office (it used to be $100 million, but so it goes). The rest of us are going to be read and evaluated in order for our scripts to make it up the ladder. Lose the reader and you get shot down. Captivate and excite the reader and you move to the next level. It's as simple as that, almost like a video game, if beating the game took three to six solid months of work, hundreds of pages of writing, and came with a potential six or seven figure payday. What follows are some thoughts and tips on how not to lose the reader. Or, put more positively, how to approach the mechanics of writing a screenplay that is compelling and engaging from beginning to end. It may sound like a tall order, but if you've been with us for the previous six chapters you have a huge leg up now that you're finally ready to begin writing. Let's start at the beginning....

The Opening

The opening to your screenplay is critically important for two reasons. You need only put yourself in the position of the audience watching your movie and the freelance script reader or development executive reading your screenplay to understand them. If you spend your hard-earned dollars to see a movie in a theater and the first image you see is a couple chatting about seemingly inconsequential matters in some nondescript location, a diner perhaps over a cup of coffee, unless that restaurant blows up within the first few minutes you're going to look at your watch and wonder why you didn't wait for this picture on streaming, or ignore it altogether. That doesn't necessarily mean you have to open your screenplay on a big action sequence or a comic set-piece — though it doesn't hurt (again, see *Raider of the Lost Ark*). But you do need to open on an image or a scene that helps draw us into the world you've created and build anticipation for what's to come.

91

The movie audience arrives excited, full of anticipation. You don't want to let them down in your first scene.

The same is true for your reader. Put yourself in their position. Your reader could be a freelancer, an agent, or a busy director looking for his or her next project. They don't know you personally; they just know someone told them to read your script. You'll probably be nervous and excited all weekend, waiting to hear what they think. They, on the other hand, will greet reading your script with a healthy degree of skepticism, maybe even dread. *Another bad screenplay, who has the time?!* Of course, it's not your fault they dread reading your script. You've written the one good one they'll read all year! But the truth is that the really good script is the exception, not the rule. Unless your reader knows what your script is about, and has been offered assurance from people he or she trusts that the execution is every bit as good as the idea, they're opening to page one with, at the very least, a fair amount of trepidation. It is therefore essential that you open your screenplay with a scene that immediately rewards your reader for giving you and your script a shot. If you're introducing the world of your movie, do it in the most captivating way you can imagine. If you're introducing your lead character, make sure that character has a memorable entrance. Your reader has seen all the movies, they've likely seen most or all of the models you've used for your script, so don't waste their time rehashing what's already been done with a familiar image or scene. Raise their eyebrows with an inventive, unexpected opening that helps to establish the world of your movie and frame it tonally and thematically. If you've taken the proper amount of time with your outline, you will already know what this scene is and how you want to approach it. But if you've written your outline in shorthand, e.g., "Open on bank robbery. ALEX chooses to shoot his fellow crew member rather than take the life of an innocent teller," you're going to have some additional thinking to do. Your "Alex" may turn out to be a compelling anti-hero, but we've seen bank robbery scenes before, even bank robbery scenes with perpetrators who are decent people at heart. Give it to us in a way we haven't seen before. Then apply that very same criteria to pretty much every scene you write thereafter.

That is how you engage and entertain your reader and your audience. With every scene, before you begin writing, you ask yourself: *What is the most interesting way I can do this? How can I do this in a way we've not seen before?*

Now, as we noted earlier, real people do have coffee in restaurants and drinks in bars. And you want to be authentic. You don't want to be clever at the expense of what's real and relatable. But if you're writing a scene that calls for your characters to have a conversation over coffee or a beer, use the opportunity the conversation itself presents to do what the setting does not. Reveal something unexpected, or in an unexpected way. Make sure it's dynamic. Treat this relatively static scene as vital, not expendable, not just in terms of the plot that's advanced, but in terms of how it's revealed. If you've done your chart and you really understand the opposing interests and perspectives of your characters you should have enough information to make any scene in your script dynamic and compelling.

The Nuts and Bolts

We're going to assume that you have a basic understanding of the mechanics of screenwriting. That is not a difficult threshold to meet. It can be accomplished by reading a how-to book that focuses on just that, like Syd Field's *Screenplay*. It can also be accomplished just by reading screenplays. That's how we did it. We didn't take a class; we didn't read a book. We just read scripts. Lots of them. Good scripts, bad scripts, scripts that had been produced, and scripts that didn't have a chance in hell of being produced — or so we thought. They all had three acts and were broken down into sluglines, action, and dialogue, just as yours will be. If you're not really familiar with the technical aspects of how to write a screenplay, we recommend going online and finding the screenplays for the movies you used for your models. Or other familiar movies. There are thousands of scripts available free online for you to learn from. Just make sure the ones you choose as your examples appear in their proper industry standard format. Or you can visit sites like The Writers Store* that sell how-to books and provide basic how-to resources for free online. What follows is a gloss on the basics that's geared specifically toward building the momentum of the screenplay and Not Losing Your Reader.

First, it's important to recognize that screenplays are intended to capture and create movement from start to finish. Remember that you're writing a motion picture. Every word you write, from your opening slugline to your final fade out (if you use such a thing, which we typically do not) should contribute to that forward motion. That means that as you establish the world of your screenplay you want to move in your format and descriptions from the general to the specific, beginning with your sluglines and continuing with your description of character and action, until you arrive finally at the words that are coming out of your characters' mouths.

Sluglines

You're going to open your screenplay and begin each scene with a slugline. If it's appropriate, and you actually have something to establish or reveal, it's often preferable to open your script in an exterior location. Moving from the exterior to the interior provides context in space and contributes to that sense of movement. Opening a movie inside can also feel claustrophobic. If that's your goal, go for it. If you're writing a horror movie shot entirely inside a house, by all means open your movie in the closet. If you're writing a western, and you want to capture

---

* https://www.writersstore.com/
how-to-write-a-screenplay-a-guide-to-scriptwriting

wide open spaces, maybe don't open inside the saloon. A movie about the Green Bay Packers might open like this:

```
EXT. LAMBEAU FIELD - DAY
```

Three elements in the slugline, that's it. Interior or exterior, location, and time of day. In production there are only two times of day, day and night. That's how movie shoots are scheduled. You can be more specific in your writing if you like — LATE NIGHT, EARLY MORNING, SUNSET — and that may help orient your reader. Just know that when the assistant director puts your movie up on a production board there will only be daytime scenes and nighttime scenes. An "early morning" scene in your protagonist's kitchen is not necessarily going to be shot in the early morning. But let's not put the cart before the horse. For now, you're writing for the reader, not the A.D., so go ahead and use whatever time of day best orients us in your story.

Now let's mix it up. Your next scene may be in the locker room, in which case you want to add one more element to the location above. You still want to establish that you're at Lambeau, but you want to set the scene in a specific location within Lambeau. So which comes first, the locker room or the building in which the locker room is situated? The answer can be found in our guiding principle of moving from the general to the specific.

```
INT. LAMBEAU FIELD, LOCKER ROOM - DAY
```

You might think you can eliminate Lambeau from the slugline altogether, as you've already established the stadium location in your opening shot, and follow with:

```
INT. LOCKER ROOM - DAY
```

But then what happens when the Packers play the Bears? Are we in the locker room at Lambeau or at Soldier Field? You can't use the same slugline for two different locations. Your reader will be confused and your production crew will want to kill you.

Character Description

Less experienced writers often fall into the trap of writing much more about their characters than they need to and than they should. Here's the thing to remember: In general, you can't shoot character description, so pretty much nothing you write here will actually make it into the movie. So why are you writing it? You do not want to go into physical detail about your characters, except to the extent that it impacts your story. Why? Because the best actor to play the character you say is overweight might be thin as a rail. The actor with the brown eyes may turn out to be better for your lead role than the actor with the blue eyes, as you've written it. If you're writing an underdog sports movie about a basketball team, it may be relevant to include the height of the players. The color of their eyes and hair . . . not so much. The smoothness of their complexion? Only if your story calls for them to be cast in a soap commercial. Characters in movies are revealed through their actions and their responses to the circumstances you put them in, not by what you write about them in description in your script. Less is almost always more. When your movie is getting made the production team will provide character breakdowns for talent agents and managers. With the exception of a character's general age range, those breakdowns will almost never be culled from your descriptions. They'll be based on the character's role in the story, their personality and attitude.

Finally, in keeping with the guiding principle of this book, look at your characters and how you're going to describe them from the point of view of the actor reading the script. These actors are your creative partners. They're going to breathe life into your characters. You want to honor them in any way you can. Don't demean them with description meant to take the place of actual insight. If the only thing you can say about a woman in your script is that she's "hot," maybe you haven't quite given that character her due? If the lead's brother is a "fat loser," you may have revealed more about yourself as a writer than you have about the character. Honor your characters from the moment they appear in your script and understand the utility and the limitations of character description.

Action

The reader's eye is moving from the slugline to the action to the dialogue. You do not want to disrupt that momentum. Action is important. A small amount of description can be important, too. But try not to overwrite. Limit yourself, for the most part, to description that can be shot. Write leanly. So instead of:

```
He reaches into his back pocket, removes his
wallet, takes out a five-dollar bill, and hands
it to her.
```

How about:

```
He takes out his wallet and hands her five dollars.
```

If you're having trouble deciding what to include and what to take out, imagine you're describing the scene to a friend. What would that sound like? There's really no reason to include more detail in the action in your script than you would in telling the story to a friend. Include the details that matter and leave out the rest.

Of course, different kinds of scripts call for different approaches to writing action and description. A quiet drama like Mike Mills' *20th*

Century Women will likely read different than the script for an effects-driven superhero movie like *Wonder Woman*. Here, too, the test of how you'd tell the story to a friend applies. *Wonder Woman* is full of high stakes set pieces in a battle between good an evil, and the tone of the description, whether on the page or in conversation, would likely reflect that. *20th Century Women* has three women of different generations wrestling with the question of what it means to raise a man. The whole movie is essentially an extended conversation, one you could imagine describing sitting on a couch over a glass of wine. The tone of the action you describe should match the overall tone of the movie you're writing. In either case, though, limit yourself to what's necessary. Remember, your reader is just waiting for an excuse to stop reading. Don't give it to them. Keep the story moving forward, reveal more and more of your characters as you go.

Finally, as screenwriter, your job is important enough. Don't busy up your screenplay trying to do the jobs of other departments. If you're not the director or cinematographer, don't call the shots. It's important to be specific about elements that add richness and texture to your characters and story. But it's important to know the difference between meaningful specificity and stepping on the toes of your director, production or costume designer, or composer. Include details that impact your characters and story and that help to capture the tone of your script. But if you direct your movie in your screenplay, instructing all your prospective creative partners in what to do and how to do it, you will have a very difficult time attracting those partners to your project. Again, look at your script from their point of view. Don't take away their opportunity to bring your story and characters to life through their talent and creativity. They know their jobs better than you do. Let them do it. Keep the action tight. Keep it moving. Continue to draw the reader's eye from the action to the dialogue, and before they know it, they'll have read through to the end of your script. Mission accomplished!

Dialogue

If you've been diligent about all the prep work you should have completed by now, finally having the opportunity to write full scenes with dialogue should be a pleasure. No amount of description in your one pager, or your chart, or your outline or treatment can capture what your dialogue will ultimately reveal, the voices of your characters come to life. If you have a reasonably good ear, and you understand the respective points of view of your characters, there's no reason you shouldn't be able to write crackling good dialogue that reflects those characters' attitudes and personalities. And that is really all you have to do. What that means, though, is that your characters should not all sound the same. It doesn't matter where or when your story takes place or what kind of work your characters do. Each character should have his or her own voice. It may take a while, even a few drafts, for you to find a character's voice, which is fine. But if all your characters speak in the same way, your script will read as monotonous and inauthentic. Here's a test: read through your scenes skipping from one line of dialogue to the next without looking at who's speaking. Can you tell which character has which line? If not, you may still have some work to do. It may have been Neil Simon who said that you should never be able to get away with two different characters swapping lines. If two characters can say the same thing in the same way, then they're essentially indistinguishable from one another. What's the point of having them both in your movie? You know your story and you know your characters. Find your way into dialogue that provides each of them with a unique voice.

Another caution: Just as you don't want to overwrite action, you don't want to overwrite dialogue. You may be able to get away with a speech every once in a while if it's truly called for, but they better be few and far between. We once worked with a producer who claimed to use a "one finger rule." She'd hold a finger to any bit of dialogue that looked long and anything that went beyond a single finger was cut.

That was enough to scare her writers (including us) into writing lean and spare dialogue.

Keep your dialogue consistent with the tone of the rest of your script. It's good to inject humor into just about anything you're writing. Almost any genre and situation can benefit from a character with a sense of humor. But if you go too broad and you're not writing a broad comedy, you're going to lose people. And "Don't Lose People" is the cardinal rule of the bulletproof screenplay.

We met when we were thirteen years old and have been best friends since fifteen. When we're together, we still have a tendency to revert back to the way we talked to each other when were kids. Sometimes it comes out in our writing and it becomes a problem. We don't always have the objectivity to tell the difference between the colorful and the absurd. It's helpful to have people you trust read bits of your script early — a first act, maybe — just to make sure the work you've put into preparation is paying off in execution.

Mostly, you want your dialogue, like all other elements, to contribute to the forward motion of your screenplay. Not just in terms of story momentum and revealing your characters, but in the enthusiasm it engenders in your reader. Think about the movies you go through life quoting with your friends — these are lines of dialogue that capture a feeling or a situation like nothing else can. Your goal is to write dialogue that feels real, that's also just a hair more clever or funny or insightful than we generally are in conversation — not so much more clever that it feels inauthentic or pretentious, just clever enough so that when folks walk out of the movie they feel like what you wrote captures their experience better than they could ever say themselves.

Finally, a trick. Your characters should not be so quick to give away what they're thinking or feeling. In life, we're rarely open and self-aware enough to share with others the complete and honest truth, especially at the beginning of a conversation or confrontation. If we were, there wouldn't be much room left for drama. It makes sense for your characters to play things close to the vest at the beginning of a scene. Maybe they have something to protect, maybe they haven't yet reached a point of self-knowledge, or maybe they just don't know how to respond to an obstacle that's been placed in their path. As a scene progresses, the natural momentum should lead toward a confrontation that exposes a central conflict and reveals some essential truth. That's the moment when you can sometimes get away with a character actually speaking in a self- aware and honest way, and it can be very powerful. Take, for example, the climactic courtroom scene of *The Verdict*, written by David Mamet based on the novel by Barry Reed.

Paul Newman, playing attorney Frank Galvin in a tour-de-force performance, represents the family of a woman currently lying in a vegetative state because, he argues, she was given the wrong anesthetic by her doctors before surgery. Galvin is losing his case, the deck having been stacked against him from the beginning. He puts his final witness on the stand, a nurse named Kaitlin Costello Price. Price testifies that under pressure from the defendant in the case, one of the most-respected surgeons in his field, she changed the admittance form *after* surgery to reflect that the patient last ate nine hours before the operation, not one, as the patient actually reported when she entered the hospital and completed the form. Kaitlin Price's testimony is like a bomb dropped in the courtroom, the copy of the admittance form she's kept with her since that day, a smoking gun. It seems Galvin has turned his whole case around with this one witness, that he may win his case. There are still some clever legal maneuverings from the brilliant defense attorney played by James Mason, but as far as the story and our lead are concerned, the scene might as well end there. And then Mamet adds a grace note that heightens the emotional impact of the scene and the entire movie. As the defense grills Kaitlin Price about why she would hold on to such a form for four years, after one of thousands of operations in which she'd assisted as a nurse in this hospital, Price recalls the threat from the surgeon that day, the day she apparently decided to leave nursing forever, and erupts in fury . . . "Who were these men . . . ? I wanted to be a nurse . . . "

"I wanted to be a nurse." It's one of the most memorable and impactful lines in the movie. The business of the scene is over, but Kaitlin Costello Price has more to say. She wanted to be a nurse, and these powerful men who told her to lie to protect themselves took that from her. Kaitlin Price appears in only a few scenes in *The Verdict*, but that honest, revealing, and anguished line packs an enormous punch.

Sometimes, when the business of your scene is over and you've accomplished what you set out to do, there's still more to say — something true and revealing, an exclamation point on your scene that comes from the most personal and heartfelt place. If you can challenge yourself to arrive at this emotional truth, you will surprise your audience and your reader, you may even surprise yourself. And you will tempt your reader to press on to see what other unexpected delights they may find in your screenplay.

Transitions and Segues

In a way, a writer moving from one scene to the next in a script is like a musician transitioning from one song to another in concert. The good and seasoned musician doesn't just come up with a setlist at random, picking song titles out of a hat. The experienced pro looks for ways to build momentum in a show by carefully crafting the best possible sequence in a set list. This is what you're doing, too, building momentum — suspense, dramatic or comedic tension, urgency. If the scene you're cutting to next doesn't create forward motion, it may be cut bait. Or maybe you just haven't arrived yet at the best way to get into it. Now is not the time for complacency. Consecutive scenes that don't build from one to the next are an open invitation to a reader to close the script and say, "I just lost interest." Where does the ending to one scene lead you in the next? Is there movement? If not, take the time now to reconsider. Don't just follow your outline on autopilot. Your reader will only meet your screenplay and your individual scenes with the energy you invest in them. Keep the bar high for yourself from page one to the very end, and in every scene and transition along the way. Reward your reader for sticking with you for the full ride and you, in turn, will be rewarded.

It's a Marathon, Not a Sprint

Back in '93, when we were writing *People of Girth*, subsisting on Subway sandwiches for lunch and mac & cheese out of a box for dinner, the apartment we shared on Stearns Drive in L.A.'s South Carthay neighborhood was like a screenwriting factory, in production almost 24/7, with time each day taken out only for about five hours of prime time and late night television. Diamond was a morning person and Weissman was a night owl. So we'd work together all afternoon, figuring out whatever needed to be done in meticulous detail. Then, after Letterman, Weissman would do his writing and leave a stack of pages outside Diamond's door, and Diamond would pick up bright and early from wherever Weissman left off the night before finishing in time to work together again over lunch. And then the whole process would start all over again until we completed a draft. As you can imagine, it didn't take us long to finish a draft of a screenplay working at that pace. Here's a list of some of the scripts we wrote during those years of struggle that felt to us at the time like Dante's Ninth Circle of Hell, but which, in retrospect, we view with some degree of fondness, even wistfulness: *Mike and Morley, The Final Solution, House Rules, Fountain of Youth, My Town, Pinkos, The Vitamin Girl, People of Girth.*

Know what all those titles have in common . . . ? We didn't sell any of them!

Script after script, knocking 'em out one after the next, typing morning, noon, and night as fast as our stubby little digits could dart around the keyboard of our Apple IIc's, and where did it get us . . . ? Eventually it got us to an agent who helped us put the brakes on, and start thinking more and typing less. That's when we sold our first spec.

Once you've vetted your idea and planned out your movie in meticulous detail, it's only natural to want to race to the finish so you can begin your career and savor the first day of the rest of your life, the day that agent calls and says, "I'm gonna sell this for a million dollars."* Or, "I can see a path to getting this made."** Try to resist that impulse if you can. As Diana Ross and Phil Collins famously sang, "You can't hurry love, you just have to wait . . . " Or, to quote the old adage in this and probably every other business, "You can have it fast, cheap, or good — pick two." The work you put into the first script you sell will be cheap. It doesn't get any cheaper than free. And it will be good. It'll have to be. Don't worry so much about fast. Get it right. Impatience is your enemy. Remember to pause before each scene to consider what will make it sing, what will make it different, unexpected, riveting, moving, hilarious, authentic, scary, inspiring . . . . Most of us who move to Los Angeles to become screenwriters can't wait to achieve the goal of officially turning professional. Recognize that if you're not very careful, chasing that desire can actually come at the expense of quality. It's a tough balance to strike, but in this period, as you're finally setting out to write your screenplay, you want to try as best you can to be both Luke Skywalker, eager to make your mark, and Yoda, the wise and patient mentor. When you feel the seemingly unquenchable desire to succeed, try to remember the powerful companion desire that fueled this pursuit from the beginning — the desire to produce in your reader and audience the very same feelings you had when you fell in love with the movies. Writing the script takes time. Give it the time it takes, even if it's hard, and you are more likely to be rewarded for having done so.

One way to keep yourself from writing like a runaway train is to begin each day by looking over what you wrote the day before, or even rereading your draft from the beginning. If this will derail your process,

---

* This doesn't happen anymore.
** This does.

sucking you into a rabbit hole and making it impossible for you ever to move forward, by all means press ahead and go back later, once you've reached the end. But rereading what you've done thus far can be one way to ease you into your writing day and keep your head in your story. It can also help you find small but significant ways to improve your script along the way. Your first pass will still be a rough pass; but if you begin each day by reading and lightly revising what came before you'll emerge with a noticeably sharper, more polished rough pass that's much closer to the target you're shooting for — with a feeling of accomplishment to match.

That's it. You've got an exciting idea, compelling and colorful characters, each of whom has their own voice and perspective on the central theme of your movie, and you're working from a bulletproof outline. You know the function each of the mechanical aspects of your screenplay will serve to bring your story to life. And you've got your head together. Congratulations, friends, you're officially battle ready. It's finally time to get writing!

Almost . . .

One Last Thing . . .

You're about to embark on a long haul. Writing a script from start to finish is a real test of endurance. Some scenes will feel great to write, others may be labor intensive, challenging, seemingly impossible to crack. First of all, don't worry. Your first pass through the script will be the first of many — too many to even count if you're truly fortunate and you're being paid for future drafts. Not only does it not have to be perfect right off the bat, we can assure you that it most definitely will not be perfect. It's okay to write scenes that are placeholders, as long as you don't *submit* a script with scenes that are placeholders. You have time to figure things out. Some things can only be fully discovered and fully figured out once you're able to actually read through a completed draft of your screenplay. That's all part of it. Hemingway famously said "The only kind of writing is rewriting," and you will have plenty of opportunities in all the rewriting ahead to nail your script and get each and every scene, maybe even each and every line, exactly how you want it before you submit your script to a producer or agent or manager.

All that said, you're going to want to gird your loins for the challenge ahead. That may mean different things to different people. To some, preparing to go into battle means three solid days of procrastination, playing online solitaire, poker or Sudoku. Others may turn to a quick trip to Joshua Tree, a new workout regimen, or making playlists to write by. Whatever works to help clear your head and strengthen you for the task ahead is worthwhile and important — and you shouldn't feel bad about taking the time to do it. For a day or two, maybe three. And then it's time to put your idea and your preparation to the test and get writing. That's right. Now. Be excited— you're about to accomplish something you've thought about doing for a long time: writing a screenplay. No, not a screenplay . . . a movie!

the bulletproof rewrite

Suppose you're buying a car — nothing fancy, just something safe and reliable to get you where you need to go. A sales rep or executive from GM approaches you and offers you a nice-looking vehicle, a brand new model that hasn't even hit the market yet and they're going to give you a great price on it. There's just one catch: It hasn't been tested yet. For anything. The prototype's been designed by a great team, put together by an expert production crew. It just hasn't been road tested or safety checked. They don't know if the seat belts work. Or the brakes. Would you buy it?

That's your first draft, a brand new prototype fresh off the assembly line. It's been carefully and cleverly designed and built to specifications in the form of your 105 page, or 130 page first pass. And no one in their right mind would buy it. It's sometimes difficult to believe, after such careful planning and preparation, and such meticulous execution, that the resulting screenplay could be anything but absolutely bullet-proof, but believe it. There may be a lot to love in that first draft. There probably is. But it's still a first draft. And as a general rule, first drafts suck. If you don't believe us, just ask someone you know and trust to read yours — a friend or family member, but *please*, not an industry contact! You'll get all sorts of feedback you never bargained for or expected . . . or wanted. Don't mistake a finished draft for a completed screenplay, suitable for submission. Writing is rewriting. If you really care about the script you're writing and the movie you hope will one day come from it, treat the process ahead, the subject of this chapter, as seriously and as diligently as you have everything that's come before. The secret to selling your script and getting your movie made is in the rewriting. Let's jump in.

Delivering on Your Promise . . . and Your Premise

The goal of your rewrite is to be able to hand your script to a reader and say with confidence, "This is the screenplay I intended. This is what I meant to do." There are a few steps to get to that point. The first involves you alone. You have to read your draft and ask some very basic questions:

- Have I delivered on the potential of my concept, really squeezed everything I could from the conflict and the stakes it set up for me?

- Does the screenplay make the case successfully for the point I set out to argue, my thesis, my theme?

- Are the characters fully realized? Does each contribute to the story as it unfolds? Is it clear how they evolve from beginning to end? Do they, in fact, evolve?

- Do the turns and escalations work in the story the way I planned, the way they need to?

- Have I met the expectations of my genre? Have I found ways and places in the script to subvert the expectations of my genre so the script feels fresh and current?

All of these questions, and others that can easily be added to the list, take us right back to Chapter One and the core of your movie idea. Character, concept, context. Have you clearly articulated the idea for your movie in the pages of your screenplay? And have you made the most of the idea in its execution, in the action and character development that plays out in your second and third acts?

Tackle your rewrite starting with the big issues and ideas and work your way down to the smaller points with each successive draft, moving, once again, from the general to the specific. You want to work toward the goal of handing your script to a friend, saying, "I've done all I can do with this on my own, I could really use an outside perspective." You can't turn your script over to someone else, anyone else, until you can honestly say that you've done all you can to deliver on your own idea. There's no question that there's always room for funnier, or scarier, or more emotional, or more suspenseful. If you're writing a comedy, you're going to want to do a joke pass. If you're writing a horror movie, you're going to want to do a scare pass. But none of those rewrites will matter if your reader doesn't understand what your movie's about, or why you made the choices you made in structure or character. Start with the big ideas. Make notes about how your story and characters measure up to the objectives you have for your script as a whole, for each act, for the individual scenes within each act. By the time you go through the entire script, you should have a very healthy to-do list. Some of the changes might be pretty major, others might be quite minor. Start chipping away at it. You're going to do a number of rewrite passes. If you're attentive to the movie your script wants to be, you'll get closer and closer to your creative goal with each successive pass. Your to-do list will get shorter. The rewrites will take less time. Let your idea serve as your North Star. Every pass is about delivering on that idea in the clearest, cleverest, most impactful way. Let that North Star guide your rewriting process until you can lift your hands with a feeling of accomplishment and satisfaction, as if to say, "It's the best I can do."

Delivering on Your Characters

Now do more. Remember your chart? It's time to return to your cast of characters and look at each scene from the perspective of each character. Have you delivered on each character's point of view? If not, here's your opportunity to amp up that scene, increase the pressure, the tension, jack up the comedy. It's only natural when writing your first draft to focus on the lead character and the A story. A lot of that first pass is, very naturally, about moving the ball down the field, keeping the story going, getting to the finish line. Take this opportunity to use your rewrite the way a coach might look at game film. Look at every player and what they're doing in every play. Is everyone where they're supposed to be, doing what they're supposed to be doing? If not, here's your chance to go back in and run the play differently to a better result.

Before Jordan Bayer took our first big spec script to the market, he urged us to do one final pass for comedy and character. He asked us to pay special attention to some of the peripheral characters whose points of view and voices in dialogue were not as clearly defined as those of our leads. We decided to cast each of these characters in our minds and use the casting ideas to guide this final pass and help breathe additional life into the script. The character who may have benefited most from this rewrite was Mrs. Thomas, the principal at the school our 12 year-old genius, Jake Rose, attended. Slacker Jake was a real thorn in her side. When he's discovered to be a genius, Mrs. Thomas is skeptical, to say the least. But once Jake proves his abilities by acing a battery of tests in her office, he becomes her new protégé, her greatest hope for restoring her school to its former glory by taking first place at the annual middle school College Bowl. Our first drafts of the script were much more focused on the exploits of Jake and his goofball friends, Fred and "The Colonel," than they were on Mrs. Thomas. But Mrs. Thomas has an arc in the movie, too. She has a point of view about Jake, and about education. She has hopes and dreams, for herself and for the school. In the beginning of the story she views Jake as an antagonist (as he does, her), but before long she sees him as an ally. When his magical gift inevitably begins to fade, Jake fears letting her down. So we set our sights, back in 1994, on the comic icon Lily Tomlin for Mrs. Thomas, and we wrote a draft that elevated not only her part, but the entire screenplay by giving a fuller, more distinct voice to her character. When Jordan read that draft he knew it was time to go out with the script. Almost twenty-five years have passed since *The Whiz Kid*, and we've never written another character named Mrs. Thomas, but we still do a "Mrs. Thomas rewrite" on every project, focusing on the more peripheral characters and making sure that each has their own distinctive point of view and voice.

The Cut Pass: Pacing and Page Count

The next thing you might want to focus on is pacing. If your draft is 93 pages, you haven't left yourself much room to cut. A 90-something page draft might be a real breath of fresh air to a reader when they pick it from a pile of a dozen other scripts, but if your 93 pages are over-written and bloated you won't fool anyone for long. Pacing is actually more important than page count. A 128-page screenplay that moves like a freight train and keeps you on the edge of your seat will always be preferable to a script thirty pages shorter that has no momentum. The longer script might even take less time to read. Cutting isn't just about lowering your page count, although that can be a valuable thing to do. Cutting is about making sure your scenes accomplish what they need to with no added fat. Most first passes have scenes in them that begin before they have to, and end later than they should. If you've got characters greeting each other at the beginning of a scene, "Hey, how you doin'?" "Good, you?" nothing is actually happening. That exchange is cut bait. "See you later." "Yeah . . . I'll catch you later." Same thing. Unless one character is about to shoot the other in the back, that scene ended for the audience before the characters said goodbye. Those opening and closing exchanges will never make it into your movie. Scenes don't really begin until a specific goal is introduced and met with either encouragement or resistance. Remember, motion pictures . . . keep it moving. Cut the heads and tails of scenes as much as you can and you'll find not only that the page count will go down, but the read will just feel so much faster because you've accelerated the pace of the action. Some scenes may have to be cut entirely. Take a look as you're going through the draft and make sure that every scene serves a clear purpose, integral to your story. If there's a scene that's in your script just because it was in your outline, but it doesn't advance character or story, that scene either needs to be rewritten or cut. It might have a great line of dialogue in it. Sorry. A great line does not justify an otherwise unnecessary scene. In fact, if the scene's not necessary, it's probably not quite as good a line as you think. The best dialogue is often a response to a challenge — whether it's "He slimed me" from *Ghostbusters* or "I'm gonna make him an offer he can't refuse" from *The Godfather*. A gem of a line in a scene that has no larger purpose or dramatic or comic tension will fall flat. Don't be afraid to "kill your darlings," as the oft-quoted expression goes. Anything you do in service of the greater story and screenplay will only benefit you in the long run.

When we were rewriting *Guam Goes to the Moon* for director Peter Segal (*Tommy Boy, Fifty First Dates, Get Smart*), he told us he thought the draft was running a little long and he was nervous about turning it in to the studio at its page count. But he also thought the script was working. He didn't want to cut anything. He didn't want to lose any of the action or any of the dialogue. This was the movie he wanted to make (Oh, Pete . . . so did we!!!), he just wanted it to be . . . shorter. So we told him, "No sweat, we can take five pages out without losing a moment of action or a line of dialogue." Pete was skeptical. And for good reason. We'd had marathon development and script notes meeting with Pete and they almost always included his editor, Bill Kerr. That was something we'd not heard of or experienced before but Pete believed having his editor in the room would save us having scenes or bits in the script that would never make it into the finished film. This movie was essentially edited before it was shot. What could possibly be left to cut?

Our secret, and it's not one we're particularly proud of, is that we have a tendency to overwrite, to be wordy and repetitive, to say in three phrases what can often be said in one. See? We knew we could cut from the paragraphs of action and description, and probably from some of the speeches in dialogue, too, without anyone noticing. After that, it's just math. If you cut just one line per page in a hundred ten page script, you've cut two pages. Well, with just a few hours work on *Guam* we could easily cut two to three lines per page, on average, without cutting any of the action or any of the jokes, and get ourselves down five pages. Which is exactly what we did. And Pete was thrilled. He got his lower page count and he couldn't figure out where we'd cut. He turned the script in and in a matter of weeks we were scouting locations and looking for actors to star in the movie.

Write leanly. And if, like us, that doesn't come naturally to you, revisit every line of your script in a cut pass. Trim your overwritten sentences and speeches down as economically as you can without compromising impact.

Once you've rewritten for plot, character, action, theme and dialogue, and you've completed a cut pass to get your page count down and your pacing just right, you can honestly hold that draft in your hands and say, "It's the best I can do . . . .for now." Remember that the draft you submit to industry professionals may be the last draft that reflects your vision alone. Once you submit your script, you are opening the kitchen door to other cooks. That can be a great thing to do depending on who the cooks are. The right input from producers and executives can help you refine your script. The wrong input can lead you terribly astray. So take this moment, when your draft is yours and yours alone, seriously. Is this the movie you wanted to write, from page one to page one hundred? If not, dive back in, maybe with the added perspective of friends you trust. If it is, congratulations, you've reached the moment you've been waiting for — it's finally time to hit "send" and get feedback from the folks who can actually help advance your script and your career.

the bulletproof submission

Have you ever seen the movie *Ishtar*? If not, run don't walk and watch at least the first half hour of one of the most deeply flawed but brilliant comedies of the 1980's, a decade that produced more than its share of great comedies. In it, Warren Beatty and Dustin Hoffman play Lyle Rogers and Chuck "The Hawk" Clarke, a singer-songwriter duo whose confidence and ambition far surpasses their talent. In one memorable scene, they stand together before a poster of Simon & Garfunkel and lament the fact that — at least from The Hawk's perspective — the only difference between the two duos is that Simon & Garfunkel have management while Lyle and The Hawk do not. This delusional pronouncement is funny when you hear it from someone else, but the truth is, at some point in the process of becoming screenwriters, we're all Lyle and The Hawk hoping to become Simon & Garfunkel.

Most of us think we need representation before we actually do. That belief is based on a mythical version of Hollywood in which an aspiring writer finishes his or her first screenplay, is immediately signed by an agent who then sells the script to a studio where, within a matter of months, said screenplay is directed by (insert name of genre specific A-list directory here). Of course we all know Hollywood doesn't really work this way and that most writers struggle for years to find representation, much less employment, and some simply never do. We survive this process, just like Lyle and The Hawk, by convincing ourselves that we are the exception to the rule — which some of us absolutely must be. A certain amount of denial, coupled with grit, determination, and self-confidence, is healthy and necessary, so long as it doesn't cross the line to self-delusion (like our beloved characters from *Ishtar*) and come at the expense of humility or the ability to learn from failure and disappointment. How do you know when it's time to get an agent or manager, and how do you go about getting one?

In a remarkable and uncanny turn, managers and especially agents have a way of finding writers just at the moment they are truly needed, that is, *the moment the writer has a script that can actually sell*. Until that time, you may find representation inexplicably and frustratingly elusive. The reason for this is not so mysterious and it takes us right back to the central argument of this book. Agents and managers, like producers and studio executives, are reading screenplays with the question *What does this do for me?* always in mind. If they can't sell it, or use it to sell you as a writer, it's unlikely they're going to pursue a conversation with you very far. If that seems crass or mercenary we can look at the same set of facts through a less cynical, more generous lens and still come out with the same result. If you give a script to an agent or manager that they don't think they can sell, they may say, as Jordan Bayer said to us so many years ago about *People of Girth*, "I'd love to help you, but I don't think I can help you *with this script*." Managers tend to be, at least by job description, more open to working with promising writers than agents, whose main focus is negotiating deals, or as Sydney Pollack playing agent George Fields in *Tootsie* puts it, "fielding offers." The truth is, most agents who are in a position to actually sell your scripts and secure employment on your behalf are not interested in writers with "writing samples." They're interested in writers who can leapfrog into the mainstream with a sellable script.

So the first question you'll need to have answered about your newly completed screenplay is, *Is this the one?* Of course *you* think it is, but you're hardly a reliable witness here. You need corroboration from people inside Hollywood. Which leads to the question many writers want the answer to even more than they want to know how they can improve their own screenplays: *How do I break in? How do I get industry professionals to read my screenplay?*

Penetrating the Barriers to Entry

Back in Chapter One we talked about how we submitted our writing sample, *People of Girth*, to twenty agents. How did we do that? How did we know, or know of, and get to, twenty agents who would read our script? It's an important question because, whether it's your first script or your twentieth, if you keep at this long enough and continue learning along the way, you'll likely arrive at the point that it's time for people in the business to read your script.

There are a few approaches writers can take to having their scripts read by people in the industry. The first and best approach is to move to Los Angeles if you're not already living here and get a job working in some capacity in the movie or television business. That job can be in production, it can be in an agency mailroom, it can be as an assistant at a production company, or as a freelance script reader. It can be pretty much anything that allows you to develop professional relationships with people in the business. Not contacts. Not connections.

Relationships. Relationships are key. You develop them by being conscientious, thoughtful, reliable, agreeable, and hard-working, even in jobs that may not appear to help you in your ultimate goal of becoming a screenwriter. If you do a good job in an entry-level position, the people you work with and for will notice you, they'll become invested in you and your success, and when they have the opportunity they will be inclined to assist you. That might mean reading your script, or passing your script along to someone else better suited to read it and offer feedback. These people are not just "contacts" or "connections," and they shouldn't be thought about or spoken of that way. They're actual relationships that you build over time through the work you do and the attitude you bring to it. Connections can sometimes lead to an introduction, but no one will hire you or represent you simply because of who you know. They will hire you or represent you because of the quality of work you do. Moving to Los Angeles demonstrates a commitment to this kind of work and puts you in the best possible position to pursue it. If you're serious about a career as a screenwriter, you should spend some amount of time living, and establishing yourself, in Los Angeles. Success as a screenwriter is not about who you know, it's about what you can do.

Having said that, while moving to L.A. and getting a job is usually the best way to position yourself to have people read your scripts, it is certainly not the only way — especially not in the connected world we live in today. There are screenwriting competitions, and while most of them barely register here in Hollywood there are some that do get attention. The Academy Nicholl Fellowship*, for example, has made an enormous difference in the lives of some of its finalists and winners. There are high-profile film festivals that also feature screenwriting competitions. Their finalists and winners may also attract some attention from Hollywood. A little-known local competition sponsored by a city or organization with limited or no ties to Hollywood may offer prize

---

* http://www.oscars.org/nicholl

money or other perks, but it's unlikely to help you reach your goal. You may be able to add a win at a local festival competition to your resume, but the screenwriter's resume is their screenplay; and no one of influence in Hollywood will read your screenplay just because it won a competition they've never heard of at a festival they've never been to.

If you don't live in Los Angeles and are not yet ready to move, you should research the most significant and highest profile competitions and enter them. You can also submit your script to be read on the Black List*, a site that aims to get the eyes of industry professionals on un-produced, and in many cases unrepresented screenplays. Bear in mind, while writing competitions and websites can sometimes provide exposure and even occasionally a path to success, it's the exception and not the rule. And your entry or submission does nothing to create or advance your relationships with people in the business. If you've written a script that is just mind-blowingly awesome, you may be able to submit that script online and find success from Omaha, Nebraska. You would also be in a very, very small club of people who did not have to move to Los Angeles to find opportunity and success as a screenwriter.

One more caution: Entering competitions and submitting your script to be read by the Black List or other online sites usually comes with a fee. That's not necessarily bad or wrong. The organizations or businesses accepting your submission have to hire readers to evaluate them and that money has to come from somewhere. But screenwriting should be a low-overhead endeavor. That's one of the few upsides to the period of struggle you're likely to have to endure — at least it won't cost you much. It can actually be very helpful and instructive to get an objective read from a professional reader on a site like the Black List, and it can be worth paying for it. But it's not worth going into debt over. In general, you're much better off becoming a part of a community of aspiring and working filmmakers and having others within that

---

* https://blcklst.com

community read your scripts, offer feedback, and pass your work along to others when the time is right.

As discussed in Chapter One, a writer just starting out is rarely in danger of having their work "stolen" by people working within the mainstream of the business. Hollywood may not be the most genteel or gentle of business environments, but it is a business in which reputation is everything. Agents and managers look for producers and executives who are trustworthy and effective. One who's known for taking ideas or money that doesn't belong to them will not last long in this business. That said, as we also mentioned earlier, it's important to protect yourself and your ideas by registering your scripts with the Writers Guild of America (WGA) before submitting them to industry professionals or to online sites or competitions. One does not have to be a member of the WGA to register a screenplay or script treatment with them. It can be done online for a nominal fee. Understand that that there may well be other ideas like yours already out there, or one day to appear on television or in the theaters. This has happened to us. It doesn't mean someone's stolen your idea, not necessarily. There are a lot of very creative people in this business and trying to get into this business. Write your best idea in the most distinctive way that you can. Share your work with confidence and without fear, but be sensible as well by protecting it using the means provided by the WGA.

We were able to submit *People of Girth* to twenty agents at agencies of all levels and sizes because one of us spent the five years before we sold our first spec working as a script reader for studios, production companies, and actors with producing deals. That was five years of experience reading scripts that ran the gamut in terms of quality, and delivering feedback that got noticed by producers and executives around town. We gave our scripts to our friends to read first. Once we cleared that hurdle, we'd pick a producer here or an executive there and ask them to take a look. No one ever said no. They knew us. They knew what we were trying to do. They saw our commitment to the writing and to the sometimes soul-crushing and repetitive grunt work that allowed us to pursue our writing. They were rooting for us. And when we finally gave them something they thought worthy and promising, they sent it along with their recommendation to agents with whom they themselves had a close relationship. This is how it works. It's not about contacts or connections, and it's rarely about competitions. It's about relationships. Start making them now, and when you produce a script that is truly bulletproof you will have people to show it to; just like we did.

They Like It, Now What . . . ?

So the time has come. You've finished your script, you've had some friends read it and they share your confidence and enthusiasm. And you've found your way to getting some industry reads. If you're truly fortunate and maybe a little brilliant, you will have landed on just the right idea at the right time and executed it in bulletproof fashion the first time out. If that's the case, congratulations, you have arrived. You can rest assured opportunity will find you. The more likely scenario, and this will happen even if you sell your script right out of the gate, is that the folks reading or buying your script are going to offer feedback. They're going to give you notes, and how you respond to these notes will determine a lot more than the fate of this one script. Knowing how to process and address script notes is a critical part of writing the bulletproof screenplay and developing a bulletproof career.

Script notes get a bad rap because oftentimes, if you take them completely at face value, they're awful. The delivery may be insensitive, they may reflect a complete misunderstanding of what your script is about, they may include suggestions that strike you as inane. Bad notes, or badly delivered notes, can be easy to dismiss, but dismissing them can be a big mistake. Readers' impressions and opinions, even poorly considered or delivered ones, provide valuable information. The trick is not to take them all at face value, but to take very seriously the information they provide. When you get a note, even a bad one, that's the reader waving a flag at a specific point in your script and telling you something didn't work for them. You lost them, at least partly. They're finding the holes in a script you mean to be bulletproof. Script notes are almost entirely subjective and you can argue with the specifics of them all you want (though you shouldn't), but here's something you cannot argue with: "Your script didn't work for me. Your screenplay didn't convince me that this was a good idea for a movie." If all you get back is "I didn't like it," well, there's not a lot for you to go on there. But if someone tells you, or if you can reasonably infer from what they tell you, that they weren't convinced by what you wrote or how you executed it, you need to figure out where you lost them and why.

Try to get a few reads so you don't rely on any one more than you should. Sometimes a reader is off. Maybe they were tired . . . or drunk. It's helpful to get some kind of consensus. But if three people tell you a certain aspect of your story doesn't make sense there's not much use telling them, or trying to convince yourself, that they're wrong. Your time and energy is better spent figuring where to go from here. Receiving notes is all about gathering the distance between where your script is today and the target you're shooting for, and figuring out how to bridge the gap. Your readers will have lots of ideas and suggestions about that. Some of them might be brilliant, a real godsend. Others will be god-awful. The challenge is to know how to tell the difference, and how to determine which notes to follow and in what way. But you are not helpless in the process. In fact, you are well-armed with a lot of useful and thoughtful preparation.

Go back to your idea. Go back to your tone. Go back to your one-pager and your chart. Do these suggestions help resolve the problems your readers have identified? Are they tonally consistent with the movie you've set out to write? If they work, great. Someone's just done you an enormous favor. The key is, don't execute a note simply because it came from a particular reader whose approval you crave. That will not get you where you need to go. What will get you where you need to go is a great idea that's delivered effectively in execution. Don't get sidetracked in the interest of being a people pleaser. Use the notes that help you write the screenplay you set out to write.

What if an agent or producer gives you a note that resonates but the solution they offer, with confidence, does not? This happens all the time. Just because someone's been very astute in diagnosing a problem with your script doesn't necessarily mean that the same person is going to come up with just the right solution. A better solution might come from another reader. Or from your roommate. Or you might be able to crack the problem yourself once it's pointed out to you. Address the thoughtful and perceptive notes you get, but don't feel compelled to do so *in the specific way you're told*. Executing poor notes as suggested is one of the most common mistakes writers make, and it's the reason a lot of very promising screenplays don't sell and don't get made. Rewriting based on notes is, or should be, as creative a process as writing a draft based on your original outline. Do not go into battle without a plan, and make sure it's a sound and carefully considered one; not just one that's reactive, based on incoming fire.

About a year after we sold and rewrote *The Whiz Kid* for Fox, we were walking on the studio lot with our *Guam Goes to the Moon* producer Mark Gordon. Mark also happened to have produced the giant Sandra Bullock/Keanu Reeves hit *Speed*. Never a shrinking violet, Mark shared with us his view that *The Whiz Kid* wouldn't get made no matter how well it was rewritten. As he explained it, our movie was about a twelve year-old, and "Twelve year-old kids," said Mark, "don't want to see movies about twelve year-olds anymore. They want to see *Speed*." He was right. We were at the very tail end of a curve with *The Whiz Kid*. The era of *Home Alone* and *Rookie of the Year*, *Goonies* and all the '80s and '90s kid-centered family comedies and adventure movies was over. Studios were luring middle and high school age kids into the theaters with bigger budget, action and effects-driven movies with adult characters at their center. Mark was probably correct that even a year after selling it, the very best re-write of our script, a total bulls-eye, wouldn't have been enough to get it made. But we never got to the point of finding out. We were undone in the rewrite process.

After we sold *The Whiz Kid* and went to the studio to get their notes for the first official rewrite, Chris Meledandri, our studio executive in charge of the project, told us our lead character Jake and his crew, Fred and "The Colonel," didn't have enough of a goal in the movie. Eventually, of course, after he becomes a genius, Jake takes on goals that others in the movie — his principal, his parents, the girl he likes — have for him, specifically, winning the annual College Bowl. Chris wanted these guys to have a goal of their own in the first act of the movie, that they could then pursue with new and more powerful tools once Jake becomes a genius. That was a good note. With time and experience we wouldn't need to be given a note like this (and now maybe you won't either), but at the very beginning of our career, we needed to be told. But Chris also had a specific idea for what that goal ought to be. A classic car. The boys want to buy a classic car. This seemed odd to us. We just didn't know, and don't know now, a lot of twelve year-old boys who are into classic cars. Sports, music, sneakers … maybe even sports cars or muscle cars … but classic cars? That felt to us like an adult passion. Now, Chris Meledandri is a really smart guy. He's gone on to make a tremendous impact on the industry with accomplishments that include the founding of Illumination, one of the most successful and innovative animation companies in the world. At the time, though, we just disagreed with his suggestion. So we put up some respectful resistance, explaining that the general note made sense but that we thought there might be a better option than the classic car. It's possible that we didn't offer a compelling enough alternative in the conversation, but our resistance was met with an uncomfortable silence, followed by a curt and very direct instruction from our producer. "It's the classic car, guys."

There are some notes you'll take that will help you enormously. There are others that will be offered that you can take or leave, or that you want to implement, just not in the precise way that's suggested to you. It takes discipline and thought to separate what helps from what hinders. And then, if you're successful and your script is in development at a studio or streaming outlet, there will inevitably be the ones you have to take because the only alternative is being fired (which is sometimes, but not usually, a better alternative). The frustration and sting of those no-win situations passes with time, aided by the fact that being in a position to be fired can only mean that you've been hired in the first place. And that is your first objective — to get in the game.

To this day — decades later — whenever we feel pressured into taking a script in a direction we feel will cost us creatively, our response in the privacy of our partnership is, "It's the classic car." At the time, that comment felt to us pretty much like the end of the world. Now, with experience and other produced credits under our belts, we recognize that the notes process calls on us to raise our creative game, and that sometimes even that will not be enough. That can make for a rough day at the office. But, once again, a rough day at the office presupposes you have a job. Keep your eye on the prize. Focus on delivering a bulletproof rewrite of your script. If and when the bad notes come, you will have those WGA health and pension contributions and a couple of fat commencement and delivery checks to console you, so . . . congratulations!

Be Strong and of Good Courage

As we look over the list of scripts we've written and rewritten over the course of our career — forty-seven projects and counting for film and television — there are many more that remain un-produced than produced. Some of those stalled projects generated greater disappointment than others, but certainly the intention with every one was to get the movie or the show made. And for it to be good. And succeed. It doesn't always happen that way. To anybody. When we were starting out, we went to hear Lowell Ganz and Babaloo Mandell give the Borowsky Lecture on Screenwriting at the Academy of Motion Pictures Arts and

Sciences. This was twenty-five years ago and the comment they made that remains with us today, perhaps more than any other, had to do with the number of un-produced screenplays they still had on the shelf. Now, these guys have a list of credits as long as your arm. They've created indelible characters, memorable set-pieces and lines of dialogue, movies and television shows that have been both highly regarded and commercially successful. No one makes everything. Not even the most talented and the most successful among us. So what's the secret? What is the secret to a successful and enduring career writing for film and television?

In a word? Resilience.

That's pretty much it. We said it in the beginning and it all comes back around to it at the end: Pursue it as long as you love it and you're not doing harm to yourself or others. Choose your ideas carefully, be discriminating, and strive to execute them in the best way possible. But understand that as important as talent and hard work are, it may be resilience that determines, more than anything else, whether or not you're successful in the long run. Our fifteen produced projects from a list of forty-seven might not sound like much. But ask a major league ballplayer if they'd settle for a lifetime batting average of .319. Screenwriting isn't like playing the lottery, it's more like playing in the major leagues. The most successful players train hard, listen to their coaches, learn from their mistakes, and know what it's like to swing and miss. Even the best in the world.

If you've come through this process with a screenplay that provides producers with a clear path to getting a movie made, chances are you'll find qualified representation, sell your script, and be well on your way to the career you envisioned for yourself. But what if you go through all the steps convinced you've written the bulletproof screenplay, and the marketplace disagrees? It's critically important to recognize that as screenwriters we can only control what we write and how we write it. That's no small thing, and there's a lot of freedom and opportunity in it. But we cannot control the marketplace or the decisions of people with bosses and boards and shareholders to answer to. There will be scripts you will not sell. When that happens, honor the disappointment; take a day or two to lick your wounds and then brush yourself off. Show your grit and determination by getting back to work on your next idea. The poet Kenneth Rexroth wrote, "Against the ruin of the world, there is only one defense — the creative act." The world was created from chaos and it often feels like it remains in chaos today. The purpose of storytelling is to create order from chaos, to provide some mechanism for understanding ourselves and the world around us. To make us feel less lost, less alone. Your stories are needed. Your writing is important and worthwhile. Give it everything you've got. Be creative, be diligent and disciplined, be ambitious, be curious and open, be generous and kind. Be the hero of the script of your own life and you will become . . . The Bulletproof Writer!

afterward

We started writing *Bulletproof* as a resource for aspiring writers. We ended up learning as much from the process as we've shared. The chapters in this book lay out an approach we've taken to screenwriting since the beginning of our career. We didn't come up with it in a vacuum, or with the idea of writing a screenwriting how-to book. We arrived at it organically over twenty years ago and we've stuck with it because it's worked for us. We don't claim it'll work for you just because it's worked for us, nor do we claim that some other writer or instructor or screenwriting guru's method won't be better for you. We offer the approach, insights, and suggestions in this guide for your consideration, in the hopes that they'll be helpful, maybe in combination with other suggested methods, or with what you're already doing. But we've noticed something both welcome and unexpected since completing the manuscript. Writing this book has made us better screenwriters.

It's true that this "bulletproof" process is one we've already followed for years. But formalizing our approach in these pages, putting in writing not only what we do and how, but *why* we do it this way, has injected a deeper sense of purpose into every aspect and stage of our writing. It's forced us to re-engage with the fundamentals. A process that was generally effective, but which had become almost rote, is suddenly subject to and invested with renewed rigor — the kind of rigor that's necessary when you're on the outside of Hollywood, trying to break in, but which can fade over time unless one is truly vigilant. We notice it as we talk about new ideas, as we craft pitches and try to crack stories for movies we want to write. Writing this book has left us thinking that anyone who does a job for twenty years or more — no matter what that job is — should consider putting in writing what they do, how they do it, and why they do it that way. Share the wealth of your knowledge and experience with others — the opportunity to reflect on it and put into words what often remains unspoken, perhaps even taken for granted, might just make you richer.

The experience of writing this book and the benefits we've already reaped are a reminder of another critical prerequisite for doing this, or any job, well: the commitment to always be learning. Every job we have, every partner we collaborate with — whether it's a producer, other writers, a director, executives, actors — has something to teach us about being better screenwriters. In 2001, we sold a project called *Piano Lessons*, based on the memoir by Noah Adams, to then Warner Bros. president Lorenzo di Bonaventura. This was the year after *The Family Man* had been released. One of the first questions Lorenzo asked us in our meeting, before any of us said a word about the project that brought us to his office, was what we learned from the process of making *The Family Man*, and from its release. He posited that every movie you make has at least one critical lesson to teach that you carry forward to every project you work on thereafter. He wanted to know what the lesson of *The Family Man* was for us*. Really, he wanted to know how what we learned on *The Family Man* might benefit us all on the project we were about to talk about together. That was the conversation that led to the sale of *Piano Lessons*, one of our all-time favorite, still-to-be-produced projects.** The point Lorenzo was making to us then, and that writing this book has reinforced for us once again, is that to be the kind of writers we aspire to be, to continue to be relevant and working at the top of our game, requires reflection, honest self-assessment, and a commitment to learning from every success and every disappointment. Writing this book has given us the opportunity to

---

*The lessons we learned from *The Family Man* could actually fill a book all their own. Some were creative, others were about the practical realities of making movies, and the business of releasing and marketing movies. We're tremendously fortunate and grateful to have had the experience.

** "'Evolution' scribes to learn their 'Lesson'" by Michael Fleming, Daily Variety, June 6, 2001 https://variety.com/2001/film/columns/evolution-scribes-to-learn-their-lesson-1117800841/

reflect on the past, to consider more deeply, deliberately, and critically the work we do today, and to approach the work ahead with greater vigilance, diligence, and conscious intent. We hope reading the book does as much for you as writing it has already done for us, and we thank you for providing us with the impetus to write it. We can share with confidence and gratitude that it's already worked for the first writers to try it — us.

Diamond (r) and Weissman (l) in Los Angeles, circa 1989. Photo credit: Jonathan Diamond

The Notebooks — As alluded to in Chapter Five, each of us has boxes of these spiral notebooks sitting in our home offices and garages, filled with ideas, script notes, outlines, and random phone numbers of people who may no longer be in the business.

REGISTRATION NO: 550192	**EXPIRATION DATE:** 02/11/99
PROCESSING DATE: 02/11/94	**EFFECTIVE DATE:** 02/11/94
REGISTRATION TYPE: Drop-off	**EFFECTIVE TIME:** 17:00:00
REGISTRATION BY: DIAMOND, DAVID 1221 1/2 STEARNS DR LOS ANGELES , CA 90035-2661	**MATERIAL TYPE:** SP

MATERIAL TITLE: CHILD PRODIGIES FOR A THOUSAND, ALEX

WRITER(S) (Charges for services in registering above titled manuscript in accordance with the provisions printed on the back hereof.)

LAST NAME	FIRST NAME	MIDDLE NAME	LAST NAME	FIRST NAME	MIDDLE NAME
1. DIAMOND	DAVID		11.		
2. WEISSMAN	DAVID		12.		
3.			13.		
4.			14.		
5.			15.		
6.			16.		
7.			17.		
8.			18.		
9.			19.		
10.			20.		

AFFILIATION:

AMOUNT OF PAYMENT: $ 10.00

TYPE OF PAYMENT: CASH

BY:

REGISTERED BY: _____

BY: *DAVID DIAMOND*
DAVID WEISSMAN

TITLE: *PEOPLE OF GIRTH*
(FIRST DRAFT SCREENPLAY)

ADDRESS: *946 N. HUDSON #4*
L.A. CA 90038

No. **488744**

Charges for services in registering above titled manuscript in
accordance with the provisions
printed on the back hereof.

DATE *MAR 5* 19*92*

REC'D. $ *20.00*

REG. BY: *DAVID DIAMOND*

AFFILIATION: _____

MAIL

WRITERS GUILD OF AMERICA, WEST, INC.
8955 BEVERLY BOULEVARD
WEST HOLLYWOOD, CALIFORNIA 90048
PHONE (213) 550-1000

BY *Reuben Beattie*

WGA Registration receipts for *People of Girth* and *Child Prodigies for a Thousand, Alex*, the screenplay that became our first spec sale, *The Whiz Kid.*

Diamond (r) and Weissman (l) on the phone with agent Jordan Bayer at the Third Street Promenade as they receive news that actor Elijah Wood has attached himself to their spec *The Whiz Kid*. Photo credit: Adam Lichtenstein

On the set of *The Family Man* (left to right): David Weissman, director Brett Ratner, David Diamond, script supervisor Martin Kitrosser, actors Tea Leoni and Nicolas Cage. Photo Credit: Barry Wetcher

On the set of *The Family Man* (left to right): David Diamond, actor Jeremy Piven, David Weissman, Brett Ratner, producer Marc Abraham. Photo Credit: Barry Wetcher

On the set of our 2005 pilot for 20th Television and CBS with the NBA's Kareem Abdul-Jabbar and Mark Jackson.

Robin Williams' final message to us, included in a bound copy of the *Old Dogs* script he sent as a gift after production wrapped, "Write On, Dude."

acknowledgments

This book would not have been possible without the friendship and professional investment of the earliest readers of the first scripts we wrote together. Special thanks to Adam Lichtenstein and Richard Shepard, to Paul Lussier, Michael Halpern, and Jamie Mendlovitz. Thanks to the folks at Robert Greenwald Productions, circa 1988, and to the producers, production company, and studio executives who were reading our scripts while we were reading and writing coverage of other writers' scripts submitted to them. Thanks to all our representatives from the beginning to the present, whose efforts have allowed us to continue doing work we love and accumulate some of the experience we're able to share in these pages. Thanks to our friends Marc Abraham, Jon Shestack, Andrew Panay, Chris Brancato and Bert Salke—producers with whom repeated collaboration has been its own generous reward. Thanks to Jonathan Diamond for his time, counsel, and discerning eye. Thanks to Ken Lee of Michael Wiese Productions for his guidance and support in the writing of this book, and to Sherry Parnes, our excellent editor. And finally, a huge thank you to our families who follow and support our exploits, including the publication of this volume, with a mixture of enthusiasm, amusement, and love.

glossary of terms

Action – Action is one of the three key elements on the page of your screenplay. As a general rule, you should only write what can be shot and you should write leanly. Your action paragraphs should drive the story forward, constantly drawing the reader's eye and interest toward the next element on your page, your dialogue.

Amp Up – You'll hear this term around Hollywood a lot. You'll hear it about comedy, about action, about conflict and general stakes in any kind of story, and it means exactly what it sounds like — turn up the volume. Make more of an impact. This can be an annoying note to get — it's so generic — but if you'd blown your reader away with your script, you wouldn't be getting it. Amp it up.

B Story – B, C, and D stories are sub-plots. It's difficult to write a movie approaching two hours in length without generating smaller stories as a consequence of your main story, or to further develop secondary or tertiary characters. It's critical that these smaller stories are linked organically to the main action and character of your movie and that they support, even advance, the story and the theme of your movie.

Buzz – Buzz is generated by a script that gets people in the industry talking. A low budget independent film can generate as much buzz as an effects-driven tentpole. Buzz is what happens when people working in the movie business discover a bold new voice, a new talent. Great buzz about a script can jumpstart a career, even if the movie is never produced.

Chart – A mechanism for tracking the way each character in your script advances through your story. A chart can be an effective tool for preparing to outline your script in a way that allows you to understand your story from the perspective of each character.

Concept – A movie concept is a situation that poses a significant, high-stakes challenge to your lead character or ensemble. A "high concept" idea is one in which the stakes for the character are so immediately apparent that the idea requires little elaboration or explanation for its dramatic and commercial potential to be perceived.

Connective Tissue – These are the scenes between your major story turns, escalations, and act breaks. The strength of a screenplay often rests on the effectiveness of the scenes between the "big" scenes where characters struggle, debate, and exert effort in pursuit of their goals.

Context – The world in which your story takes place. The context of your story is a critical factor in communicating the very idea for your movie. It helps determine genre and stakes. Your ability to create a clear and meaningful context for your story is a significant factor in establishing your authority and your voice as a storyteller.

Coverage – Script coverage is a brief report generated by a professional script reader, or story analyst, whose job is to summarize your screenplay and evaluate the quality and effectiveness of its various components — concept, character, storyline, and dialogue. A new writer's script will often be "covered" before a producer, executive, or agent consider even reading it.

Cut Pass – A last step before submitting a script. An opportunity to make certain you've been as economical as possible in every aspect of your writing, from descriptions of characters to whole scenes that may not contribute to the forward motion of your story. A thoughtful, discriminating cut pass lowers your page count and helps the pacing of your script.

Dialogue – There are only three major elements on a page of a screenplay — scene headings, or sluglines, action, and dialogue. Dialogue should be lean and crisp and should reflect, with unique and compelling personality, the perspectives of the characters that populate your story.

Execution Dependent – Another term that gets tossed around Hollywood a lot (often as an excuse from someone who doesn't want to develop your idea or buy your pitch). It means that the concept you're pitching is so specific that if you don't execute the idea just right, there's no clear path left to make the movie. However, well-done execution-dependent ideas can thrive in the indie world even as they have become virtually extinct at the traditional movie studios.

Genre – Understanding how your screenplay will be classified and what tradition of movie it falls into is key to delivering on the expectations readers will have of your script, and subverting those very same expectations. Know your genre — the conventions and the language of it — so you can find ways to advance and challenge it.

Lead Character – Your lead character should be one who stands to gain or lose the most through the situation in which you've placed them. Lead characters should be likable and strong, with a distinctive voice and perspective, and they should be flawed or incomplete in some way. A character with no room to grow or be tested will not engage readers of your script or audiences watching your movie.

Logline – A logline is a sentence that encapsulates your movie idea and communicates its genre. Loglines are written by story analysts during script coverage and by marketing people attempting to attract interest in your movie in thirty seconds or less. They are intended for coverage (reader reports), movie listings, and submission letters. They are almost never an effective pitching tool.

Meld – A process in which each character's journey is integrated into the central story beats of your screenplay. A proper and effective meld ensures that each character gets their moment, that they don't disappear from the action, and that your script benefits from multiple perspectives and voices. It's also an effective tool for developing a dynamic outline for your script.

Models – These are the movies you'll look to for guidance as you develop and write your script. They will provide valuable information, lessons, and inspiration. They are also critical to understanding the tradition within which you're writing, and the ways you can add something new to what's come before.

Notes – Getting notes is an essential (and unavoidable) part of the process of developing a screenplay and getting a movie made. It can also be painful. And they come from everywhere — managers and agents, producers, executives, directors, actors...you might even get notes from your script supervisor. Understanding how to hear notes, use the information they provide, and address them most effectively is key to producing your best work, building relationships in Hollywood, and having an enduring career as a screenwriter.

One-Pager – The broad strokes of your story laid out on a single page. It is the basic roadmap for your movie that sets out in three acts where you're going and the essential stops along the way. A rock solid one pager ensures that your story won't go off the rails as you expand to a full outline. It's also an excellent tool as you pitch your movie idea to friends and colleagues, gauging the effectiveness of the story you've conceived and hope to write.

Outline – Your outline combines all the major events of your story with the role each character plays, and incorporates specifically *how* these events will transpire and how your characters are impacted. A good outline allows you to wake up in the morning feeling confident and excited that you know what you're going to be doing and how you're going to do it. And it still leaves plenty of room for the "special sauce" that will make your writing and your script so distinctive.

Pacing – How slowly or quickly your script moves to the reader is a critical factor in its journey from one reader to the next. 17th Century costume dramas are not expected to be paced like action movies, horror movies, or comedies. Know the expectations of your genre. Generally speaking, your script should *move* so that your reader can be moved by it.

Polish – This is your last full writing step, your opportunity to dot your i's and cross your t's, to view your story from each character's perspective, and make sure you've delivered for each and every one of them. It's your chance to catch typos and other small errors that might indicate to your reader that you're not sufficiently invested in your script or how it's perceived by professionals. It's your chance to sharpen your dialogue and make sure you've made the most of every moment. You only get one chance to make a first impression.

Reversal – An unexpected story turn that forces your character(s) to reassess their goal and how best to achieve it. Reversals provide necessary obstacles and challenges to characters and they help keep the story fresh and engaging for readers and audiences. Even the quietest of movies have unexpected turns that force their characters to reassess, regroup, and press on.

Rewrite – Recognize that your first pass at your script will likely be unreadable to anyone but you. Without seeing how your story plays out start to finish in script form, you cannot honestly assess the strengths and weaknesses of your story and characters. Your first pass is just the beginning. Your rewrite is your opportunity to use the information your first draft provides to produce a true, well functioning rendition of your story.

Rough Draft – Also sometimes referred to as a first pass (a "first draft" is actually the version of a script that's officially submitted to a studio or other buyer). This is the draft you first produce from your outline or treatment. See *rewrite*.

Runner – A motif, a "bit" that crops up periodically throughout your script, often to inject comedy and relieve tension. Runners add a layer of detail and flourish that can help distinguish your screenplay, and you as a writer.

Set Piece – Set pieces provide, in a single scene or sequence, proof in action of the potential of your movie idea. They mine the opportunities your concept provides for dramatic tension, comedy, or action. They give readers something to talk about and provide marketing executives material for cutting trailers. Well executed, buzz-generating set pieces help sell your script and your movie.

Slugline – It's the first line you'll write in any screenplay, and the beginning of each scene thereafter. Sluglines establish the time and location in which your scene takes place. Like most aspects of your writing, they should be succinct, moving from the general to the specific, always guiding the reader further and deeper into your story.

Spec Script – A screenplay written to be sold after completion. Sometimes they sell, more often they do not. A script that does not sell can still serve the writer as a writing sample, a calling card script, if it demonstrates talent and a unique voice. A particularly strong writing sample can attract representation — an agent or manager — and can be used to secure a writing assignment wherein the writer is guaranteed payment to write a script. It should be noted that writing assignments are not as common or plentiful as they once were, and representatives will always gravitate to scripts they believe they can sell over those they cannot.

Story Beat – A story beat is an event that moves both plot and character forward. Movies are not simply a series of events. Plot and character must be inextricably tied for a screenplay to have any impact on its reader.

Tentpole – Typically based on IP (intellectual property), material from another medium — comic books/graphic novels, books, television shows, podcasts, magazine articles, etc. — tentpole movies are big-budget, larger-than-life stories with eye-popping visual effects. Currently, tentpole movies drive the traditional studio movie business as they promise international appeal and the box office receipts to go with it.

Theme – Your screenplay is a debate between or among the deeply held convictions and belief systems of your characters. The prevailing belief system, challenged throughout your screenplay, is the theme of your movie. Know it. Be able to articulate it. Believe it. Feel passionately about it, and it will translate into a powerful screenplay.

Three Act Structure – The three act dramatic structure has been the foundation of dramatic writing for millennia. The first act is the dramatic expression of your movie idea. The second represents its consequences, complications, and rewards. The third is the resolution. (If that sounds simple, try recreating Coca Cola from the ingredients listed on the can.)

Voice – The unique style you bring to your writing, often captured in dialogue but found anywhere the writer's imagination can be seen and accessed in your story and your screenplay. Hollywood is constantly in search of new and original voices capable of delivering entertainment for mass consumption.

Tone – The attitude and mood of your screenplay. It should be clear and consistent with your genre. A clearly established tone will guide you as you consider lines of dialogue and whole scenes or sequences that might need to be cut, rewritten, or reconceived.

WGA – The Writers Guild of America. The WGA East and West protect and promote the interests of writers creatively, financially, and in a variety of other areas. The WGA negotiates the Minimum Basic Agreement — the collective bargaining agreement that defines terms of employment between writers and the guild signatory companies (including movie and television studios, networks, production companies and other financiers and distributors of content). The WGA also provides registration services for writers wishing to protect their rights once they've completed a treatment or script, regardless of whether or not that writer is a WGA member. There is a wealth of information about the guild and about screenwriting on the WGA website.

Writing Sample – See *Spec Script*

summary points and suggested exercises

chapter one: movie ideas

Summary Points

- Don't set out to write a screenplay. Set out to write a movie, and understand the difference.

- A complete movie idea consists of a character, a concept, and a context. Make sure the idea you're pursuing includes all three components, carefully conceived to yield maximum impact and opportunity for drama, comedy, action, etc.

- Vet your idea with trusted friends, family members, and colleagues to help determine whether the idea you're pursuing is one that will generate interest and enthusiasm from buyers and audiences.

- Understand where your idea falls in the landscape of movie distribution. Is it a studio movie, an indie, a streaming movie? Understanding your screenplay's place in the world is critical to delivering a script that meets the expectations of your buyer and distributor.

- Know as much about yourself as a writer as you can before you settle on the idea you're going to write. While there are always exceptions, you are most likely to write best and most effectively the kinds of movies you most like to watch.

Suggested Exercises

- Make a list of your favorite movies—as long a list as you can. Consider and make notes about the common elements, the themes, the genres, the kinds of characters and situations you're most drawn to, and why. Doing this before you begin brainstorming new ideas can help direct you in your search for the idea you're most interested in pursuing.

- Before you settle on one idea to write, try coming up with a menu to choose from. Take a weekend, a week, a month, and brainstorm as many ideas as you can. Make a list. Three ideas, five . . . ten. Give yourself options. The idea you ultimately settle on might be one that comes indirectly from a long conversation generated by the seventh idea on your list.

chapter two: models

Summary Points

- Your goal in writing your screenplay is to add to the ongoing, ever-evolving conversation taking place in the movies. Movies that sell and get made tend to offer a new twist, a new perspective or approach to what's worked in the past. You cannot offer a new perspective or approach unless you're intimately familiar with what's come before. Be film literate; know your stuff.

- Your goal in identifying and watching, or re-watching, movie models for the script you're writing is to contribute something new; not to repeat what's already been done. Finding models is not about discerning a formula, or copying the good work of others, it's about gathering information and inspiration that will help guide you toward distinction and excellence.

Suggested Exercises

. Make a list of models for your idea — movies from your genre, movies with a similar lead character or situation, movies that explore a world similar to the one in which your story takes place.

. Note what works and what does not about the movie models on your list. Record in a dedicated notebook or folder on your computer any useful and relevant information each of your movie models provides as you continue to refine your idea and your approach to it.

chapter three: one-pager

Summary Points

. Before you set out to write, or even outline your movie, provide yourself with a very basic roadmap of your story in the form of a "one-pager," the major turns, reversals, and act breaks in your story.

. Understanding and abiding by the time-tested rules of basic story structure is essential to writing a successful screenplay.

. Your movie is not just telling a story; it's making an argument, positing a thesis. Mine your character and your concept to identify your thesis — your theme — if you do not know intuitively what it is.

. Once you've laid out your story on a single page, you should be able to vet not only your idea, but the structure of your entire movie across three acts. Take advantage of that opportunity to test your structure for weaknesses and flaws.

Suggested Exercises

- Return to your favorite movies and identify their act breaks, story reversals, and major turns. Train yourself to think in terms of story structure and to identify and appreciate the mechanics of the movies you watch as they unfold.

- Pick one or more of the movies on your list of models and create a one-pager for each that serves as a basic road map to their story. Repeat this exercise with:

  - Movies that have stood the test of time, the iconic movies from within your genre and from outside your genre.

  - Movies you see week-to-week that really work. The exercise of repeatedly writing the essential beats of a successful movie on a single page will reinforce your understanding of and sensitivity to structure, and help you to craft simple, clear, high stakes stories.

chapter four: characters

Summary Points

- The characters you create are essential to delivering the message of your movie. You cannot prove your dramatic thesis, or deliver on your theme, without the right characters as effective messengers.

- Your lead character should be the one who is most tested, and ultimately most impacted, positively or negatively, by the situation you've placed them in.

- You cannot progress to production without lead characters actors want to play. That means creating characters who are flawed, or incomplete, but *likable*.

- Each character in your screenplay should have a position or point of view relative to your dramatic thesis. Each is either a supporting or opposing force in the journey of your main character or ensemble.

Suggested Exercises

- Return to your models. Follow the characters in the movies that are providing you with inspiration and note their strengths and weaknesses; note the difference between their stated goals and what it would require for them to be truly complete, i.e., the difference between what they want and what they *need*.

- Now turn to your movie. Go through your list of characters. Record in your notebook or folder where each stands with respect to your dramatic theme or thesis, whether they are a supporting or opposing force to your lead, and how.

- Create the chart for your movie, tracking each character — their response, their perspective, and the implications and consequences for them at each major turn in your story.

chapter five: outline

Summary Points

- Your outline provides you with a detailed, comprehensive game plan for writing your movie. It includes not only what happens and to whom — your plot — but *how* it happens. The more detailed an outline you create, the more liberating and fun your scene writing will be.

- Used properly and thoughtfully, the connective tissue in your script — the scenes between your major reversals and turns — can contribute as much to character and plot development, and to the audience's investment in your story, as your most significant story beats and act breaks.

- Subplots — B and C stories — provide an opportunity to bolster your story by filling out the lives of secondary characters with their own objectives and obstacles, and challenging or supporting the action and the theme of your A story.

- Find opportunities to break tension and make your script and movie more fun by adding comic runners and comedic voices through some of your ancillary characters.

- The outline that will ultimately serve as the blueprint for your screenplay will combine the information on your one-pager and your character chart with your connective tissue. It will also answer the question, "What happens next?" with what happens and *how*.

- The outline you write should be the one that will be most helpful to you when you enter the scripting phase. Script treatments and pitch documents may be useful as a reference tool for others who are helping you develop your script, but they will not sell your screenplay before you write it.

Suggested Exercises
- Pick a movie that's inspired you and choose a section of it to outline — the first act, the third act — or outline the entire movie. Take note of what you choose to include of the finished product and what you leave out of your outline. The outline for your movie should also look like this.

- No more delaying the inevitable, use all the information and resources you've accumulated to this point and write the outline for your bulletproof screenplay.

chapter six: set pieces

Summary Points

- Almost all movies distributed theatrically and on streaming have set pieces, regardless of scale or genre.

- Set pieces serve many functions:

  - They demonstrate and further the promise and potential of your movie idea.

  - They broaden and deepen the impact of your story.

  - They help generate buzz for your movie, both in script form and in distribution.

  - They help marketing departments sell your movie.

- Setting a scene in front of a large audience does not automatically make it a set piece.

- Producers and executives looking for "trailer moments" in your screenplay will likely find them in your set pieces.

Suggested Exercises

- Watch the trailers for the movies listed among your models. Can you imagine the trailer for your movie before you write the script?

- Consult your list of models and identify, from memory if possible, set piece scenes and/or sequences from these movies.

- Go through each act of your outline. See if scenes and sequences from your script can be elevated and amped up into a set piece where one did not exist before.

- Start incorporating ideas for set pieces into the way you share the idea of the movie you're working on, and see if listeners respond. Do your set piece ideas help advance your story, are they a distraction from it? Vet your set pieces as you would any other piece of your screenplay, refine and tweak as needed and use the best of the best in your screenplay.

chapter seven: screenplay

Summary Points

- Consider your opening very carefully — this is your opportunity to introduce us to the world of your movie, to captivate your reader and your audience, to draw us in and get us invested in what's to come.

- Always remember you are writing a motion picture; keep it moving...

- Your number one objective in what you write and the way you write it: Don't lose the reader!

- Contributing factors to losing your reader include (but are not limited to) extra fat in the story and within scenes, characters and character beats that turn your reader off, writing in a cumbersome style, grammatical or spelling errors that show you're not professional or sufficiently invested in your own product.

- Before you set out to write each scene, consider how the scene can accomplish even more than the role designed for it in your outline. How can you surprise yourself and your reader and audience?

- Think of your screenplay as an extended concert set list, designed to carry its momentum from the moment the curtain rises to the closing credits.

- Be patient, with yourself and with your writing.

- Be diligent. Write on a consistent schedule taking the task seriously.

- Give yourself a short time to procrastinate before writing to clear your head, and prepare yourself mentally for the weeks- or months-long adventure of writing your script.

Suggested Exercise

- Return to your list of movie models. Find the screenplays (most should be available for free somewhere online, through your local library, or for purchase on Amazon and other sites). Read these and other scripts written by established, successful writers. Note their style, their technique. Learn from master teachers through their work and incorporate the lessons they have to teach into your own.

- Write your screenplay.

chapter eight: rewrite

Summary Points

- Don't submit your script until you've done the best you can. If you're not yet proud of what you've written, rewrite it. Again. If you don't know how, ask for help, but only after you've done all you can on your own and you're proud of your effort.

- Hold your draft to the tests set up in previous chapters, e.g., have you made the dramatic argument you set out to make? Does each character shine throughout the screenplay and have a moment to truly distinguish him or herself? Does your script read even better than your idea sounds?

- Take the opportunity to amp up conflict, set pieces, ancillary characters who may provide comic relief or other forms of color to your screenplay.

- Cut your script down for pacing and for page count. No one wants to read a 135-page screenplay. And they probably won't.

Suggested Exercises

- Choose a scene from your screenplay, any scene. Print the scene and take a red pen to it, looking in particular for places where you can say just as much in fewer words. Writing leanly, in dialogue and in action, helps page count, pacing, and increases the impact of almost everything you write. When finished, return to the opening scene of your script and repeat this process for this and every scene thereafter.

- Read your script out loud, or better yet . . . have others read it aloud to you. You will find errors and potential improvements you never could have imagined through your own silent reading.

155

chapter nine: submission

Summary Points

- The best agent in the world cannot sell a script that a buyer does not believe they can market to an audience.

- Worry more about getting your script right than getting representation. Representation will be available to you if and when you really need it; once you've written a script that presents a clear path to production, and likely not before.

- If you need a day job while you're writing (and even if you don't), consider an entry-level position in the movie business. The closer you are to the center of the movie business the more opportunities you'll have to submit your material, and the more people you'll know who can offer you meaningful feedback.

- Screenplay competitions, festivals, and screenplay-centered websites can be good places to submit your completed screenplay and get feedback, but make sure they're reputable before submitting, and that your rights are protected.

- You should not have to pay more than a nominal submission fee to have your script read and evaluated. And you should never pay an agent, manager, producer, or film executive to read your work.

- Always be open to constructive feedback, even if it isn't delivered with sensitivity. Evaluate notes based on the extent to which they serve your idea, your characters, your story, your theme.

- Don't dismiss notes just because you don't agree with your reader's solution. Consider where your reader had a problem and why, and find another way to address their issue if you don't like their solution.

- The work you've produced en route to writing your screenplay — your chart and your one-pager — can be excellent resources when considering which notes to incorporate and how. Use them to help guide you as you address notes and come up with fixes.

- In the end, resilience is critically important to a successful writing career; perhaps even more important than talent.

- Remember that screenwriting is like any other creative endeavor. Frustration and disappointment are an inevitable part of any writing career. Honor the disappointment when it comes, give yourself reasonable time to experience it and recover, then dust yourself off and get back in the game. We need you and the stories you have to tell . . .

set piece illustration:
breast pump sequence from *Paternity Leave*

INT. PAIGE'S HOUSE, KITCHEN - LATE MORNING

Jake has a coffee mug in hand. He searches for milk in the
fridge but there is none. Finally, he spots a bottle of
Paige's pre-pumped milk. He thinks a moment, then grabs the
breast milk and is about to pour it in his coffee when...

                PAIGE (O.S.)
        Do you have any idea what I have to
        go through to get a bottle of that?

Jake's startled, then turns...

                JAKE
        How would I have any idea about
        that? Seriously.

Then, out of nowhere Paige starts crying.

                JAKE (cont'd)
        Oh Jesus. Okay, I'm sorry. I won't
        use your breast milk in my coffee.

                PAIGE
        What's the matter with me!? I'm a
        respected professional. Please
        don't tell anyone what I've become!

Elaine enters with Shelby, sees Paige crying, glares at Jake.

                ELAINE
        Nice going.

                JAKE
        That wasn't my fault, she hates
        herself.

Paige cries even louder, Elaine gives Jake another look, then
guides Paige out.

                ELAINE
        We're going shopping. We'll be back
        by 1.

                JAKE
        I'll count the minutes.

They leave Jake. He puts the coffee mug down when he sees a
BEER in the fridge and grabs that instead. He searches for a
bottle opener, then the cabinets. He comes upon...

Paige's BREAST PUMP...it's a double pumper with a clear
plastic bottle attached to each of the suction cups and a
toaster sized electric pump. He examines it...

> JAKE (cont'd)
> I don't know what she's complaining
> about. This doesn't look so bad...

He takes the machine along with his beer into the den.

Jake sits, plugs the machine in. He turns it on, it makes a
loud SCHLOOSH-SCLOOSH-SCHLOOSH sound that Jake finds
instantly amusing. He starts experimenting with the machine,
turning it on and off, then picking up the suction cups and
feeling their power against his hand, his cheeks. He thinks a
moment, checks the front door, then...

...he takes his shirt off and attaches the suction cups to
his nipples.

> JAKE (cont'd)
> Tingly.

He lets them work a minute, pumping away at his nipples. He
looks down at the suction cups, mesmerized by their motion.

He shakes himself out of it then turns on the Dodgers game
which is about to start, opens the beer and leans back...

> JAKE (cont'd)
> (mimicking)
> Do you have any idea what I have to
> go through to make a bottle of
> that?
> (back to his voice)
> Yes Paige, I happen to know exactly
> what you have to do. And it feels
> terrific!

He takes a swig of the beer.

> CUT TO:

INT. PAIGE'S HOUSE, DEN - THREE HOURS LATER

Close in on the TV: The Dodgers are up in the top of the 9th.

Pull back - Jake's in the same position except he's now fast
asleep, the machine still pumping away at his breasts.

The front door opens and Paige enters with her mom and Shelby
carrying some shopping bags. They see Jake...

> PAIGE
> No...!

Jake wakes up...he looks down at the pump.

                    JAKE
          Wait...no. I can explain...

He jumps up but the suction cups stay attached to his nipples
and the weight of the machine pulls him back down...

                    JAKE (cont'd)
          Ow!!

                    ELAINE
               (glares at Jake)
          You sicko...!

                    JAKE
          No, it's not like that! I was only
          trying to empathize with her so she
          wouldn't throw shit at me anymore!

But, as Jake goes to remove the suction cups, they all
simultaneously see something that stops them in their tracks.

<u>Each of the collection bottles have about 3 and a half ounces
of breast milk in them...</u>

A moment as they all process this. Then...

                    JAKE, PAIGE, & ELAINE
          AHHHHH!!!!!

                                                  CUT TO:

INT. CEDARS SINAI EMERGENCY ROOM - LATER

Jake being treated by a DOCTOR, Paige in the room with him.

                    E.R. DOCTOR
          ...you see Jake, male lactation,
          though little known, is actually
          quite possible with the right kind
          of sustained stimulation of the
          mammary glands and in situations of
          extreme stress. It's actually
          common among prisoners of war...

A SNICKER from Paige. Jake shoots her a look.

                    E.R. DOCTOR (cont'd)
          Expect those nipples to be sore and
          protruding for a few weeks...

We pan down to Jake's chest - you can see his nipples are
engorged and sticking out a good inch from his chest.

                    JAKE
          Well what the hell am I supposed to
          do in the meantime?!

                    E.R. DOCTOR
          Don't worry, I'm going to have you
          fitted for a protective device...

                    JAKE
          A what?!

                    PAIGE
          What are you about a B-cup...?

Jake shoots her another look.

about the authors

David Diamond and David Weissman's partnership is rooted in a 30-year friendship that dates back to their high school days together in Philadelphia. They parted company for college while Diamond majored in Cinema Studies at NYU and Weissman studied Chinese history, first at Hebrew University in Jerusalem and then at the University of Michigan. Weissman received two Masters Degrees in the subject; one from the University of Wisconsin and the second from Brown University, before setting aside academic aspirations to join Diamond, who had settled in Los Angeles to pursue a career in screenwriting.

The partners sold their first spec script to 20th Century Fox in 1994. They followed with a series of original ideas for comedies, including their first produced credit in 2000, Universal Pictures' *The Family Man*, starring Nicolas Cage and Tea Leoni. Collaborations with producer-director Ivan Reitman and producer Andrew Panay followed, yielding Diamond and Weissman's next feature credits, the

Dreamworks Pictures sci-fi comedy *Evolution*, and Disney comedies *Old Dogs* and *When In Rome*.

The team sold their first television pitch to 20th Television and CBS in 2005. More pilot sales followed for both half-hour comedies and one-hour dramas. Together, Diamond and Weissman have sold pilots at every major network, and conceived and contributed to over a dozen movies with a combined box office gross of over a billion dollars worldwide.

Now in the third decade of their writing partnership, Diamond and Weissman continue to explore concept and character driven stories that add up to more than the sum of their parts.

Contact us at: bulletproofscript@gmail.com
www.bulletproofscript.com / www.diamondandweissman.com
Twitter and Instagram: bulletproofscript
Facebook: Diamond & Weissman

SAVE THE CAT!®
THE LAST BOOK ON SCREENWRITING YOU'LL EVER NEED!

BLAKE SNYDER

BEST SELLER

SAVE THE CAT!.
The Last Book On Screenwriting That You'll Ever Need!

BLAKE SNYDER

He's made millions of dollars selling screenplays to Hollywood and now screenwriter Blake Snyder tells all. "Save the Cat!®" is just one of Snyder's many ironclad rules for making your ideas more marketable and your script more satisfying – and saleable, including:

· The four elements of every winning logline.
· The seven immutable laws of screenplay physics.
· The 10 genres and why they're important to your movie.
· Why your Hero must serve your idea.
· Mastering the Beats.
· Mastering the Board to create the Perfect Beast.
· How to get back on track with ironclad and proven rules for script repair.

This ultimate insider's guide reveals the secrets that none dare admit, told by a show biz veteran who's proven that you can sell your script if you can save the cat.

"Imagine what would happen in a town where more writers approached screenwriting the way Blake suggests? My weekend read would dramatically improve, both in sellable/producible content and in discovering new writers who understand the craft of storytelling and can be hired on assignment for ideas we already have in house."
    —From the Foreword by Sheila Hanahan Taylor,Vice President,Development at Zide/Perry Entertainment, whose films include American Pie, Cats and Dogs, Final Destination

"One of the most comprehensive and insightful how-to's out there. Save the Cat!® is a must-read for both the novice and the professional screenwriter."
    —Todd Black, Producer, The Pursuit of Happyness, The Weather Man, S.W.A.T, Alex and Emma, Antwone Fisher

"Want to know how to be a successful writer in Hollywood? The answers are here. Blake Snyder has written an insider's book that's informative – and funny, too."
    —David Hoberman, Producer, The Shaggy Dog (2005), Raising Helen, Walking Tall, Bringing Down the House, Monk (TV)

BLAKE SNYDER, besides selling million-dollar scripts to both Disney and Spielberg, was one of Hollywood's most successful spec screenwriters. Blake's vision continues on *www.blakesnyder.com*.

$21.95 · 216 PAGES · ORDER NUMBER 34RLS · ISBN: 9781932907001

THE MYTH OF MWP

In a dark time, a light bringer came along, leading the curious and the frustrated to clarity and empowerment. It took the well-guarded secrets out of the hands of the few and made them available to all. It spread a spirit of openness and creative freedom, and built a storehouse of knowledge dedicated to the betterment of the arts.

The essence of the Michael Wiese Productions (MWP) is empowering people who have the burning desire to express themselves creatively. We help them realize their dreams by putting the tools in their hands. We demystify the sometimes secretive worlds of screenwriting, directing, acting, producing, film financing, and other media crafts.

By doing so, we hope to bring forth a realization of 'conscious media' which we define as being positively charged, emphasizing hope and affirming positive values like trust, cooperation, self-empowerment, freedom, and love. Grounded in the deep roots of myth, it aims to be healing both for those who make the art and those who encounter it. It hopes to be transformative for people, opening doors to new possibilities and pulling back veils to reveal hidden worlds.

MWP has built a storehouse of knowledge unequaled in the world, for no other publisher has so many titles on the media arts. Please visit www.mwp.com where you will find many free resources and a 25% discount on our books. Sign up and become part of the wider creative community!

Onward and upward,

Michael Wiese
Publisher/Filmmaker